THE WRONG OF RUDENESS

THE WRONG OF RUDENESS

Learning Modern Civility from Ancient
Chinese Philosophy

Amy Olberding

OXFORD
UNIVERSITY PRESS

OXFORD
UNIVERSITY PRESS

Oxford University Press is a department of the University of Oxford. It furthers
the University's objective of excellence in research, scholarship, and education
by publishing worldwide. Oxford is a registered trade mark of Oxford University
Press in the UK and certain other countries.

Published in the United States of America by Oxford University Press
198 Madison Avenue, New York, NY 10016, United States of America.

Library of Congress Cataloging-in-Publication Data
Names: Olberding, Amy, author.
Title: The wrong of rudeness : learning modern civility from ancient Chinese philosophy /
Amy Olberding.
Description: New York, NY, United States of America : Oxford University Press, [2019] |
Includes bibliographical references and index. |
Identifiers: LCCN 2018056206 (print) | LCCN 2019019556 (ebook) |
ISBN 9780190880996 (Online content) | ISBN 9780190880972 (updf) |
ISBN 9780190880989 (epub) | ISBN 9780190880965 (cloth : alk. paper)
Subjects: LCSH: Courtesy. | Philosophy, Chinese. | Philosophy, Confucian.
Classification: LCC BJ1533.C9 (ebook) | LCC BJ1533.C9 O43 2019 (print) |
DDC 177/.1—dc23
LC record available at https://lccn.loc.gov/2018056206

1 3 5 7 9 8 6 4 2

Printed by Sheridan Books, Inc., United States of America

For my parents
Mike and Kay Olberding

CONTENTS

CONTENTS

PREFACE

My plan for this book began some years ago, and the book, as I then conceived it, was to be quite different. I aspired to write a book focused solely on good manners, the mundane interpersonal business of ordinary life most often addressed in etiquette manuals. Then the 2016 US presidential election happened. Every election generates political incivilities and civic discord, but in this case they did not abate in the postelection period. Instead, fierce and unsparing political incivility has become an abiding constant—it too is now the mundane business of ordinary life. Because of this, my original plan for a book on manners came to seem quaint and insensate, a book that would require a different sort of world to write. So I dropped it. Some months later, under the encouragement of Lucy Randall, now my editor at Oxford University Press, I picked up the project again, but with an eye more turned toward civic life as we now know it.

I feel obliged to confess, here at the outset, that the book is uneasy in what it offers. Never have I written a bit of philosophy so regularly challenged and tested by the world around me. I would draft material advocating seeing the fineness in our relations to others while, like everyone else, seeing so much that is not at all fine in our civic relations to each other. I would be dwelling on the need to be generous and humble in how we evaluate others while sorely tempted to find terribly many others just awful. I would be aiming for the confident optimism this book ultimately advocates while trying mightily not to succumb to the despair and alienation our age so well encourages. And, in truth, I wrote haunted by the thought that even recommending good manners is, in the current civic climate, a view that can be despised, a view that can invite just the denigration and insult so characteristic of our present culture. To call for greater peace is to invite the storms of war in one's direction, I fear.

Ultimately, this book is a record of struggle more than anything else. Indeed, while writing it, I often thought of a particular Buddhist injunction. The *Dhammapada*, a foundational text in early Buddhism, suggests that one way to quiet enmity is to recognize, "We here are struggling." While this book leverages much of its thinking from a different philosophical tradition, early Confucianism, I think the Confucians would have appreciated this Buddhist strategy, and it operates as an undercurrent in the book. *We here are struggling*. This registers for me both the context in which the book came about and the great uncertainty I bring to it. I think that many in our civic life *are* struggling and that the struggle at least partially consists in trying to hang on to the shreds of a civic "we" who can meaningfully struggle together. Or at least in seeing that our fellow citizens, most especially those who disagree with us, struggle too.

In an effort to capture the sensibility of common struggle, I have deliberately adopted what some may find too light a touch where political and civic disputes are most heated. I have tried to aim for a discussion of civility and manners that can register struggles across the political spectrum. I have, in short, sought to speak beyond my own moral and political convictions precisely because my more earnest and urgent desire is to speak well and humanely with those who do not share them. There is much in our current life that makes this desire hard, and this book is, in many respects, an effort to make it a little less so.

ACKNOWLEDGMENTS

This book elaborates and provides a personally engaged account of research that I originally developed in several previously published academic journal articles and online sources. These earlier articles are "Etiquette: A Confucian Contribution to Moral Philosophy," *Ethics* 126.2 (2016): 422–446; "It's Not Them, It's You: A Case Study in the Exclusion of Non-Western Philosophy," *Comparative Philosophy* 6.2 (2015): 14–34; "From Corpses to Courtesy: Xunzi and the Defense of Etiquette," *Journal of Value Inquiry* 49 (2015): 145–159; "Confucius' Complaints and the *Analects*' Account of the Good Life," *Dao: A Journal of Comparative Philosophy* 12.4 (2013): 417–440; and "The Moral Gravity of Mere Trifles," *The Forum: Thinking in Public* (http://blogs.lse. ac.uk/theforum/meretrifles/), published May 29, 2017. These earlier works adopt the conventions and aims of professional academic scholarship. Here I try to touch the rubber to the road, speaking not of how ideas operate in philosophical ethical systems, but of how they operate in me, a person who simply wishes to be better than she is.

The work of writing this book has been supported by many. My academic institution, the University of Oklahoma, provided me with an Arts and Humanities Faculty Fellowship and research sabbatical to provide sustained time for writing. I am also grateful to several institutions that hosted me to discuss the work and, especially, to their students, who often offered questions and insights that greatly profited my own thinking. These include Skidmore College, University of Richmond, Rogers State University, North Dakota State University, and Columbia College, as well as OU's own Institute for the Study of Human Flourishing. The much-maligned millennial generation I have encountered in my own teaching and in visits to other campuses has been a heartening and generous resource as I have thought through the themes of this work.

I am also grateful for the support I have received throughout the process of bringing this book to print. My editor Lucy Randall and Steve Angle of Wesleyan University both provided feedback on the book's first draft that substantially improved it. I am also grateful to Hannah Doyle, Raj Suthan, Melanie Johnson-Moxley and Richard Isomaki for their work in managing the always complicated business of getting a book manuscript between covers and out into the world.

Finally, my family has been a substantial resource. My husband Garret and daughter Adelein were steady sources of inspiration and good humor. Garret, as he always is, was my first and best reader, ready to see what I meant and help me say it even when I was flailing. Adelein kept me more current than I might otherwise have been with how ordinary life looks from the standpoint of the young. My parents, Mike and Kay Olberding, and my uncle, Don Prantl, read drafts of the work. My father, in particular, notified me when my sentences were too long or my tone too lofty. Where more typical evaluators might label a sentence merely "unclear," he would crunch the numbers and note in emphatic horror: "This sentence has 67 words!" Any sentences in this book that remain too long will not be his fault. Above all and far more importantly, my family models much of the humane generosity I seek to advocate in the book. A core element in this book is the desire to thrive with and among other people, and I recognize my good fortune in having a family that makes this a happy desire easy to fulfill with them.

THE WRONG OF RUDENESS

Chapter 1

Introduction

Because this is a book on good manners and civility, it might seem natural to begin by decrying the sorry state of our political discourse and interpersonal interactions. I could, for example, observe the ever-worsening decline in civility, lament the youth of today, pine for the way things used to be, or launch some telling anecdote that captures in miniature all that is presently so wrong with the world. I assume, however, that readers can supply this predictable beginning for themselves. I want instead to focus on truths that, for me, are closer to the bone and less often addressed than the sorry state of our culture. Here are those truths: I am often rude. I often *want* to be rude. I often *enjoy* being rude. I even frequently enjoy witnessing the rudeness of others. Indeed, I could write a book devoted entirely to rudeness I have relished. Much of this rudeness would be political and tied to the present state of the world, but once I begin to catalog happy moments of rudeness, the types multiply. They include, for example, the sweet relief that comes from taking out frustration upon others, the liberating thrill of abandoning care for others' good opinion, the indulgent delight of expressing irritation at any who obstruct my will, and naughty pleasures derived from seeing those too big for their britches humbled. Indeed, one of my earliest childhood memories is of the ribald joy I achieved the first time I flipped someone off. My target was a neighbor child who, in my view, had long richly deserved it owing to a tendency to lord over the rest of us his vast and incomparable wealth of Lego sets.

In addition to enjoying deliberate rudeness quite a lot, I should also allow that I am rude far more often than I intend to be. Quite apart from my conscious moments of rudeness, I also inflict rudeness on others by accident. My greatest vice on this score is interrupting when others are speaking, a habit that bespeaks an impatient temperament, one comically at odds with another of my vices, an academic's tendency to hold forth too long and overtax any poor soul obliged to listen. These are impolite tendencies I recognize in myself, though no doubt my friends, colleagues, and students could supply more. I am unhappily confident that I daily inflict rudeness of myriad sorts on others who have the misfortune of encountering me. Absent conscious awareness of it, I commit a host of crimes and misdemeanors where well-mannered social conduct is concerned. Since I am not aware of these as they transpire, my guess is that they replicate exactly those forms of unpleasantness I encounter in others, others who, like me, simply fail to pay attention, suffer from poor habituation, or incompletely conceal what they really think when their private thoughts are indeed quite rude or disrespectful.

In scrutinizing my own tendencies toward rudeness, whether intentional or accidental, I notice that being polite is a kind of labor and that rudeness often has the character of respite or release. Being rude can be an interlude of rest from the arduous work of social cooperation and the feigned agreeability it often requires. Unintentional rudeness often arises in moments of relaxing slack in the taut attention social coexistence entails. Deliberate rudeness provides the chance to set down the taxing burden of hiding what I really think or feel. That being rude is so easy and sometimes feels so exquisitely good owes, in other words, to the pains induced by polite restraint. Good manners have a long and storied association with the beautiful, but rudeness, I must admit, can be sublime. Its pleasures emerge in the kinetic transition: from labor to rest, from burden to lightness, from bondage to freedom, from the itch of insincerity to the scratch of honesty.

Being polite is a pain, and rudeness is remedy and relief. However, not all pain is bad for us and not all relief is good. In this book, I want to argue that the pain of politeness is *worth it*, that it is better to be polite than not, even, and maybe especially, when it hurts. In taking this view, to be clear, I seek to convince myself as much as any reader. We may often have high expectations of those who enjoin us to good manners. Traditional etiquette writers, such as Emily Post, are classy practitioners of the art. Political theorists enjoining us to better conduct in our civic affairs are comfortable extolling the noble ideals of robust democratic processes and public reasoning. I can play neither of these roles naturally or easily. Where class is concerned, I come from folk at ease with eating messy sandwiches over the sink; where civic life is concerned, I confess to having fire-starter impulses, sympathy with the socially disruptive and suspicion of where civic restraint leaves the least of us. My arguments thus have about them a self-therapeutic quality and represent the sorts of considerations I aspire to bring to bear in guiding my own conduct. While I will probably always enjoy some rudeness, I want to like it less. Perhaps more to the point, I think there are good and formidable reasons to suffer the pains of politeness, and it is these I seek to offer in what follows.

Many of the arguments I offer take shape under the influence of the world's most ardent advocates for civility and good manners, the Confucians of ancient China. There is much, I think, that recommends their work to our attention. The early Confucians lived in terrible times, when internecine violence and political conflict in early China were peaking (sixth to third centuries BCE). Feudal warfare throughout this period rendered the fundaments of life, such as security and meeting basic material needs, vulnerable and fragile.

Where our own political climate may incline us to find polite practices prim or altogether too precious, the Confucians suggest otherwise. Confucian injunctions to civility do not flower from naive or romantic assumptions about humanity, but are instead hammered on the anvil of political struggle and personal suffering. The Confucians do not simply suggest that one needs good manners in political and personal turmoil, but insist that this is when one needs them most. Theirs are good manners for the clever and fierce, for those astute about how power and conflict work in the world and seek to bend it toward justice.

Even as the Confucians operate with high ambitions about what civil practices can do politically and socially, they begin with the premise that the first front in any battle for a better world is improving myself. They astutely recognize that what I will find in the world will be influenced by what I bring to it. Likewise, they recognize that modeling the improvements you want to see in the world can help bring those improvements into being. These are their highest aspirations and they ride on the hope of making a difference by being different oneself. Significantly, these optimistic imaginings are coupled with a heady realism, a willingness to recognize that even where one hopes for better, sometimes the best one can do is to do one's best. Thus while cultivating my own capacity for civil conduct reaches for a world in which respect for others and social relations flourish, even if this cannot be achieved, there are consolations in trying.

What most recommends the Confucians, however, is their devotion to *both* civility and good manners. The Confucians did not distinguish political civility from ordinary, interpersonal good manners. Both were captured in the term *li* 禮. *Li* is often translated as "ritual," but it enfolds far more than this English term does. *Li* included not only everyday etiquette, but also governed political affairs, religious ceremony, and mourning rites. *Li* thus regulated routine polite conduct that would shape daily social intercourse and also ordered momentous human experiences, occasions in which doing things right would have high moral, instrumental, or emotional priority. Part of what unites these various forms of experience is their repeatability. Social experience includes commonplace patterns, and *li* represented collective wisdom about how we can best navigate these patterns, whether they concern, for example, political disagreements or entertaining guests in our homes. Most importantly, the Confucian fusion of political civility and personal good manners better tracks what human experience is *like*. Arguments to this effect are implicit throughout this book, but because a first step in self-improvement is knowing one's target, let me explain my use of the familiar English terms I will employ in place of *li*. Although many of the terms I will use are familiar, I will not be using some of them in the usual ways.

Throughout much of this book, I will be using "civility" and "good manners" interchangeably. This, I own, is a move likely to inspire early frustration in philosophically trained readers, readers who are primed to want ever more distinctions rather than fewer and who will immediately declare that being civil and being polite are different. It is likewise at odds with much in popular discourse, for in contemporary Western culture, we do often conceptually distinguish civility from good manners. A canvas of any bookstore's offerings will quickly illuminate the difference. Works on civility will be placed in sections devoted to politics and public life. Works on manners will, in contrast, detail rules of etiquette, and will be found among the self-help and do-it-yourself books. Civility is the stuff of political theory, concerning ambitiously high values such as tolerance in pluralistic, democratic societies. Good manners are the stuff of domestic life and interpersonal relations, concerning rules for navigating the myriad intricacies of ordinary life. In contemporary America, if you want to read about the conditions for thriving political discourse, you will want books about civility; if you want to read about interacting sociably at dinner parties, you will want an etiquette manual. This book will insistently fuse the two for the most basic reason: the distinction between civility and good manners is an artificial intellectual conceit that is simply not native to the wilds of actual life.

In my own experience, I struggle to separate those occasions in which I need political civility from those requiring interpersonal good manners. Our high political and civic ideals are not decoupled from even mundane domestic interactions with kin and acquaintances. This, I expect, is readily apparent to anyone who spared a thought for what Thanksgiving dinner would be like after the most recent US presidential election. Sitting at table mere weeks after the election with kin and companions who disagreed politically inspired dread in many. Such is to say that ordinary domestic life has us regularly in contact with matters political. This is a rather self-evident truth, but there are more subtle truths in our experience. Even our most ostensibly apolitical encounters have about them elements of sociopolitical life. Everyday interpersonal conduct may, without our conscious awareness, embed a host of social biases rooted in the political and economic arrangements of civic life. If I am rude to a store clerk, for example, my disregard for her feelings and willingness to speak disrespectfully emerges from a system of class arrangements that enable my rudeness to pass without penalty. We are more free with our rudeness to store clerks than we are to those enjoying greater social status, to those socially empowered to answer in kind or hold us to account. Indeed, the division we in the West make between political civility and systems of etiquette is itself an intellectual intervention brought about by class consciousness. We did not always divide civility from good manners, and the way they historically came apart is instructive.

The conceptual divide between good manners and civility emerges from literary social history, from the appearance on the book market of etiquette manuals that detailed, in fine and excruciating detail, the rules of polite society. Historian Michael Curtin traces the development of the contemporary etiquette manual to shifting economic patterns that began in the late 18th century and rapidly gained force in the 19th century.[1] Increased economic mobility meant that many from the "lower orders" achieved the financial wherewithal to enjoy privileges previously reserved for the few. Long-standing class structures were not, however, merely financial, and one could not simply buy one's way into better society or purchase social standing. For that, one needed command of the refined behaviors of the better sort. Thus the etiquette manual was born. In it one would find instruction pitched to provide those newly blessed with financial capital the means to achieve corresponding social capital. What society's higher orders could do effortlessly, the newly rich had to acquire through self-conscious study, and etiquette manuals provided the tuition they needed. The most ardent students of these works were women and this too was a function of shifting economic realities. That women were the primary audience for etiquette manuals would also function to decisively separate good manners from civility.

Curtin argues that the 19th century saw a "feminization" of etiquette, a gendering of good manners that is still with us today, though the conditions that produced it have long since passed. As many families saw improvement in their economic fortunes, the women of these families began to enjoy an unprecedented level of leisure. Able to afford paid help to accomplish much of the household's domestic labor, women of newly prosperous families had more time for other pursuits, and they turned their now less calloused hands toward contributing to the family's social fortunes. Mastery of etiquette—becoming adept at entertaining, paying calls, and performing the niceties once reserved for an elite—was a new form of domestic work and instrumental to the family's fortunes, both social and material. Through skillful social activity, women could forge social connections that would afford their children opportunities previously denied and profit a family's business interests. Etiquette manuals aimed to school the uninitiated in the mysteries of high social conduct. They thereby allowed women to seize a form of power in steering family fortunes, but they likewise indirectly confessed the limitations of this power.

The largely female audience for the etiquette manual was a population without power in public, civic life, and indeed part of being a well-mannered woman included maintaining a distance from political life. A 19th-century etiquette manual thus would not instruct women on how to express political disagreement politely or school them on conversationally navigating controversial public issues. That is, it would not talk about civility, for the simple reason that if one ought not have political opinions, one need not learn how to express them respectfully. The narrow focus on domestic life that so shaped the etiquette genre was driven by the narrowness of the lives of the genre's target market. One consequence of this, as Curtin shows, is that etiquette books were treated by the intelligentsia as a "despised and trivial genre."[2] These books detailed often tedious rules for entertaining and superficial social agreeability divorced from the nobler, more muscular work of genuine public life. The legacy of this separation of etiquette and good manners from civility abides with us still, as does a certain intellectual contempt for writing on etiquette. Still notably feminized, our etiquette manuals sit in the bookstore alongside even more emphatically feminized books, such as those on home decoration and wedding planning. The word "etiquette" is itself sometimes rejected as useful for discussing serious subjects, something I quickly learned in trying to write for academic philosophers about etiquette. Among my readers' responses were protests against using such "ladylike" language and concerns that talk of etiquette is inherently "prissy."

While the legacy of feminized etiquette is still with us, the world in which this made a certain sense has long passed. Both men and women participate in public, civic life; both have need of interpersonal social skillfulness. The boundaries between domestic, private life and civic, public life are soft, if they exist at all. Perhaps most of all, as the Confucians would insist, we can hardly expect to be masterful at political civility where we are lousy with interpersonal good manners or to excel at politeness with our immediate companions where we are rude when engaged in politics. For the skills informing good manners and civility grow from a common root, emerging from attitudes we adopt about the worth and value of other people and the worth and value of life with others. How, then, might we define them with reference to this common root? What exactly are we doing when we are "polite" or "civil?"

For an initial working account of civility and good manners, I find it most useful to think of them as behaviors that symbolically demonstrate prosocial values. These values include some of our most ambitious moral values—respect, consideration, and toleration—values we might consider the firmament of shared moral life with others. And it is typically these values we find violated in rudeness and incivility. Thus, for example, if we disagree politically and I announce that this owes to your being simply too dull-witted to discern the truth, I have violated these values. I decline to recognize your rational capacities to hold the views you do, fail to consider your feelings upon being insulted, and evince an unwillingness to grant that intelligent people can hold differing views; I am disrespectful, inconsiderate, and intolerant. Crucially, it is not simply that I believe you to be dull-witted, but that I *say so*. As the contemporary philosopher Cheshire Calhoun argues, civility and, I would add, good manners involve "display."[3] They concern how we *perform* values and communicate them to others.

Once we recognize that civility and good manners are matters of performance and display, we are obliged to consider *how* the values they represent are displayed. Clearly, I will fail at being civil if I perform my respect or consideration in ways that you cannot recognize. This is where etiquette comes into view. "Etiquette," as it is commonly defined and as I shall use it throughout this work, refers to the *rules* and *codes of behavior* that operate as a kind of social language. Where civility and good manners describe the *what* that we seek to communicate, etiquette describes the *how*, the rules of behavior we follow, the scripted speech we employ, and even the habitual gestures we undertake. Thus, if I want to show consideration upon receiving a gift from you, the familiar script of "thank you" provides a reliable and recognizable way to do so. Likewise, if I fail to say "thank you," you may well and reasonably conclude that I have failed in consideration for your effort and beneficence. Feeling gratitude is important, of course, but expressing it in the ways we commonly recognize is key to your knowing that I feel it, to your feeling appreciated and acknowledged. Because of this, to talk about civility and good manners—those broad and ambitious big values—requires talking about etiquette—the rules that structure our ability to get our big values out into the world where others will see and recognize them.

The case I want to make in this book, then, is that we need to do *all* of the hard work. We need to cultivate the wide values embedded in civility and good manners, and we need to shape our conduct in accord with etiquette rules that facilitate communication of these attitudes. Willingness to do this work, to conclude that the labor is worth it, hinges in part on dispelling the temptations of acting otherwise. Incivility and rudeness *are* quite appealing, and never more so than in social and political contexts like our own, where disagreement is intense, where coarse insult frequently supplants reasoned discourse, and where fellow feeling with opponents is minimal. So the first step in encouraging good manners and civility is getting a handle on the attractions of their opposites.

Since we do, in a contemporary idiom, keep civility and manners distinct, the ways we describe the appeal of these reflects the distinction. The reasons we give for being uncivil are often cast in the lofty language of public goods and social ills, while our reasons for being ill-mannered or rude concern our relations with immediate others and how we believe those relations should go. So let me retain this distinction a little longer and address the temptations as we typically tend to describe them, keeping civility and manners distinct just the way our popular reasoning does.

Chapter 2

Temptations to Incivility

Civility, as it is currently understood, concerns public life and discourse. It governs, or should govern, how we interact about issues of moment in our lives as citizens and members of a society we inhabit and shape together. Most discussions of civility naturally center around disagreement, and for good reason. Living in a pluralistic, democratic society entails that we share public spaces and common resources with many who will not hold our views and values. Civility is a mechanism for managing difference and disagreement, for guarding common life against fractious and destabilizing conflict that could undermine it. However, I will emphasize disagreement for the far more immediate reason that although I want generally to be civil, abiding by norms of respect and toleration is hardest where I encounter opposition to what I personally judge right or good: I am most tempted to incivility with people who disagree with me. Advocates for civility would say that this is when I need civility most, but of course it is also when I want it least. Some of the reasons for this are quite basic.

To be uncivil in disagreement is to communicate disrespect, intolerance, or inconsideration, and, let's face it, we will often feel that an opponent deserves this. So at a rather brute level, incivility is a refusal to conceal. I opt to say what I *really* think or feel about another's views, values, or even person. This is why we sometimes defend incivility by claiming to be "telling it like it is," implying that in incivility we but publicize, unchecked and unamended, what is already transpiring in our internal responses to others: Do I seem to disrespect you? Well, that's because *I do.* This is of course heady, appealing stuff, particularly when we have long held ourselves in check, where we have labored hard to keep our disrespect under wraps. To be, at long last, *honest* can register as potent relief. This is one of the great pleasures and attractions of incivility, but there are others.

Incivility can be gratifying for reasons beyond its felt liberation—after all, the habitually uncivil do seem to enjoy themselves even though they suffer least under civil restraint. Here too, there are rather brute and basic forces at work. Incivility can afford a host of goods, both personal and social. Incivility can be funny and entertaining. Mockery is an especially effective tool for delivering disrespect, and incivility of all sorts is often delightfully incongruous. It defies our expectations regarding how interactions typically proceed and thus can seem a refreshing and pleasantly shocking departure from the ordinary. Incivility can also feel quite empowering. This owes in part to its "honesty," but also to its potential to win attention and approval from others. In my incivility to you, I may say what many think and they may thank me for it, praising me for what I say or do in disrespecting you. More cynically, incivility can be a way of triumphing in debate, not by winning in a contest of ideas but by reducing my opponent. Incivility can be a social dominance strategy, with uncivil speech or gesture conveying that my opponent is someone unworthy of the usual courtesies, much less attention to her ideas. I can try to discredit a point of view by disrespecting the one who holds it.

Whether we look to incivility's purported honesty, its potential for comic relief, or the social power it can bring, the appeal of incivility is here attached to pleasures it affords. It can feel good to speak one's mind, to laugh, to win approval, to diminish or dominate those who disagree with me. Yet these features of incivility are rather atavistic in their appeal. They explain why incivility can feel good, but we often conclude that pleasure, in the full measure of things, ought not drive our behavior. Since civility concerns how we conduct shared life with others, my personal enjoyment of incivility seems a rather juvenile and self-indulgent reason to be rude. And I think, perhaps optimistically, that this is rarely all that drives us when we choose to greet disagreement with incivility. The baser joys of incivility may be a kind of bonus, but the most compelling temptation to incivility, for me at least, concerns how incivility can seem, on balance, morally good and right.

When I most powerfully want to be uncivil, it is because I think incivility is *morally better* than civility. Sometimes, I think, in order to be good, one cannot be nice. Indeed, our strongest political and philosophical arguments against civility circle around just this: Civility may be a general good, but there will be times when incivility is better, better for individual persons and for society writ large. The impulse to incivility may sometimes track genuinely moral needs and interests incivility could help address. Getting a handle on the nature of this temptation—what it includes, how it works, and whether it ought be resisted—is thus crucially important. If we want to be more civil because we want to be *better people*, we need to know what to do when it seems that the temptation to be uncivil is a moral pull. Our current public and political discourse suggests that this is a temptation widely felt.

Several recent social media memes insistently declared that it is morally justifiable to "punch a Nazi."[1] Nazis, several suggested, have no rightful claim on respect, nor can the social compact to tolerate others' values cover their views. Some views simply reside beyond the pale and, crucially, incivility helps keep them there, in social exile. However much we generally prize respect and toleration, we want to be able to draw a line, to acknowledge that some views simply do not, and justly cannot, require this of us. Even the most civil among us will sometimes want to drop social nicety and verbally, if not physically, punch. And, if our target *needs* "punching," our incivility will be both socially salutary and morally honorable; our rudeness will be righteous. Righteous rudeness, in this line of argument, notably favors shared morality and the public good. For incivility toward Nazis is an example of incivility turned toward preserving existing social values and norms. Excepting the radical few, society has collectively repudiated the rancid racist ideology of the Nazi. Thus when we decline to grant the Nazi among us respect, we rehearse and reinforce values that socially bind, effectively saying that our collective commitment to respect *for all* morally requires signaling our disrespect *for him*. Cases such as this serve to remind us that however committed we are to civility, our commitment cannot be total. It may go too far to say we ought physically assault the Nazi, but we need not, and morally *should* not, treat him as normal.

Incivility has much to recommend it when civil toleration would undermine values we have collectively resolved to be correct, but cases like this are comparably rare. Far more often, the temptation to morally motivated incivility will not have the crisp purpose of upholding long-standing public values. Incivility can play defense and guard important existing social values, but it is more often employed on offense as we use incivility to promote values we do not already collectively share or values society professes to hold but fails to honor: Rather than defend a status quo that is good, I use incivility to challenge a status quo I find bad. It may be the case that my society treats as "normal" views or practices that I find morally wrong; the social consensus is one I personally oppose. More commonly, society may simply lack any stable public consensus about a moral matter. We have settled together against the Nazi, but there exist vast reaches of civic life that are not like this. I may well know what I value, you may well know what you value, but *we*, as a society, remain in disagreement. In such cases, civility itself can operate as a kind of status quo that my own moral sense will tempt me to violate.

The traditional case for civility would hold that where value questions remain socially unsettled, we should resist the temptation to assert our own views uncivilly. We should instead opt for open debate guarded by civil norms that prevent disagreement from descending into fractious turmoil or even violence. The goal of civility in this context is that all behave in ways that allow conversation to continue in the belief that shared deliberation is to the public good. We want to form robust, collective consensus, and the path to this will run through dialogue that respectfully entertains the views and values of all involved. This general case for maintaining civility in service to dialogue and consensus building seems prudent and sensible. Nonetheless, I may well find that society treats as unsettled an issue that I simply and steadfastly cannot. That is, ongoing civil exchange over the issue seems itself deeply wrong to me. For example, if society is unresolved over whether women enjoy the rationality necessary to vote, it seems to require inhuman heroism (or, worse, abject self-abnegation) to insist that women gamely and respectfully debate their own rationality with skeptical others. The suffragettes, bless them, were rude and we think now that they were onto something with that, that acting as "well-behaved women" would have delayed or impeded important social progress.

Because history does offer examples in which violating existing civil conventions favored and perhaps hastened the development of new and *better* public values, righteous-seeming temptations to incivility are not well answered by simply urging respectful dialogue. Indeed, exhortations to respectful dialogue are sometimes used to keep the morally helpful boat rockers and fire starters among us quiet. For the command to "be civil" can operate as a way to insist that we accept the world just as it is, without protest or complaint. Much incivility is inherently socially disruptive, yet we can have compelling reasons to think that society *needs* disruption, that the way things are should not be left unchallenged and undisturbed. The suffragettes thought so, and indubitably the uncivil among us have sometimes operated as moral beacons, their refusal to politely engage lighting the way to a better moral world. It thus seems reasonable to think that incivility against common consensus or in defiance of "ongoing dialogue" can be on the side of the moral and social good, that it too can be righteous. However, while righteous incivility in defense of shared moral consensus entails standing with others and for our common values, righteous incivility in political dissent and social criticism involves choosing to stand apart from my social peers or my society writ large. Because of this, the decision mechanisms of critical righteous incivility are different and bear closer scrutiny.

At issue in righteous incivility that breaks with prevailing social norms is the way we can experience a gap between what our society treats as acceptable and what we personally judge acceptable. Cheshire Calhoun describes these personal judgments as the "socially critical moral point of view."[2] What she captures with this idea is that mature morality entails more than blunt conformity to the norms of one's society; it requires forming considered independent judgments. And these independent judgments will, inevitably, sometimes lead one to conclude that society has got it wrong, that some prevailing collective norm is not morally correct. Likewise, independent judgment often works to settle issues that society persists in treating as open and unresolved. We may have no shared consensus on issues that, for me, my own moral sense has firmly settled. That I have moral views opposing my society's or that I have settled for myself some of society's "open questions" does not, absent other conditions, tempt incivility though. I can, after all, have my own judgments and express them civilly. What, then, are the additional factors that will make critical righteous incivility seem the sometimes better course? Some of the possible reasons are practical and some principled.

To be uncivil is to break with social norms we expect to be in operation, to step outside the typical, expected ways of speaking and behaving. Because of this, incivility arrests the attention of others. Used in social dissent or criticism, it can forcefully summon others' attention and, it is hoped, provoke them to consider its underlying moral reasoning. The drama of an uncivil gesture may thus act as a social alarm, alerting others to ills that they have failed to notice or startling them out of complacent acceptance of the status quo. Critical righteous incivility can also be deeply expressive. What works as an alarm can also function as a distress signal, with incivility communicating moral injury, outrage, or despair. Violation of our civil norms can announce that all is decidedly not well with us or with some of our members. Where social ills treated as acceptable are especially egregious, incivility may bespeak a depth of injury cooler civil expressions cannot well convey, and as others witness what the righteously uncivil person feels, they too may come to feel it. Righteous incivility, then, can operate not just as a moral wake-up call but as a call to moral-emotional arms. In either case, as a practical matter, whatever social good civility might usually do for us, sometimes greater social good arises from incivility. And the appeal of critical righteous incivility only gains force when we consider what it can feel like from the inside.

If I possess deeply held moral convictions that civility would require me to suppress, suffocate, or stifle, I may decline to do so in order to preserve my own integrity. This can be existentially quite important. Deciding to stand apart in favor of personal conscience can be seen as self-preservation: How can I be the person I aspire to be if I act tolerant in circumstances I find profoundly morally objectionable? How can I hold myself in moral esteem if I betray my convictions in order to be socially agreeable to others? Critical righteous incivility may thus be a potent refusal to morally self-sacrifice, to preserve, whether in fact or aspiration, values identified as essential to one's sense of dignity and integrity. The righteously uncivil person, then, may decline society's superficial tokens of civil respect because her own moral self-respect demands it.

Whether I am motivated by practical effects, personal integrity, or both, critical righteous incivility can look quite compelling. Indeed, considerations such as these almost convince me that we need not resist the temptation to uncivil expression of deep moral convictions, that critical righteous incivility is a simple and straightforward good. But only *almost*. Discerning readers may have noticed that I have been rather spare in offering examples of critical righteous incivility, dwelling largely in abstraction. This, I confess, is deliberate. For making judgments about particular cases of critical righteous incivility carries us into thickets of complexity and complication. One rather fundamental complication is that just as our independent judgments about moral issues will vary, so too will our opinions about what properly counts as *righteous* incivility delivered in dissent or criticism.

Consider two quite uncivil examples. A Democratic advocate for wider health care coverage greets Republican plans entailing reduced coverage with the uncivil hope that this will increase death rates among Republican voters: "I hope Republicans get their way," he says, "because then I'll enjoy watching them die as preventable diseases ravage the Republican uninsured!" In similar fashion, a Republican opponent of gun control greets advocates for stricter laws with the uncivil hope that they will be defenseless under threat: "Let gun control advocates get their way," he says, "because then I'll enjoy watching them die as criminals ravage their undefended homes and persons!" Incivilities of this sort are an increasingly common element in our contemporary public debates. Significantly, both examples openly and gleefully wish ill on opponents—they are formally just alike in this—but my guess is that most people will react more negatively to one than another. Even if we find both problematic, few are likely to find both *equally* so. Instead, our political beliefs about what is right regarding the underlying issues will enormously influence our reactions, rendering us more likely to excuse, forgive, or even admire incivility when it favors our own views. What I evaluate as a case of admirably righteous incivility may strike you as garden-variety belligerence or wrong-headed, unhelpful social aggression. Which of us is correct? I naturally believe that I am, and this, I think, indicates a real challenge where my own decisions to engage in critical righteous incivility are concerned. My habits with respect to the incivilities I admire in others make me doubt that my own temptations to critical righteous incivility are as noble as I would like to believe.

My readiness to count the uncivil righteous, I confess, largely tracks whether the uncivil agree with me; I like best just those incivilities that enact my own moral judgments. The incivilities I find morally brave, commendably independent, and socially useful will be just those—let's face it, most often *only* those—put in service to values I hold. In contrast, incivility delivered against what I hold valuable will register as objectionable, offensive, or plainly wrong, and the transgressive pleasure of watching the mighty fall diminishes dramatically when the mighty are my own moral compatriots. Thus I am forced to the unhappy suspicion that what I want to call "righteous incivility" is all too often just socially pugilistic enactments of my own values. I do not like critical, morally motivated incivility; I like seeing my opponents felled. Rather than admiring a righteously uncivil person's exercise of social dissent and personal conscience, I may be just celebrating exercises in tribalistic schadenfreude, delighting in me and mine taking down you and yours. Because of this, I begin to worry that my temptations to "righteous incivility" contain much that is brute, my uncivil impulses driven by the baser delights rather than the high moral purpose I want claim for them.

It is of course tempting to think that a little tribalistic schadenfreude may be forgiven so long as I belong to the right moral tribe: If I fight on the side of justice, surely I can enjoy getting in some licks on justice's behalf. But this thinking just pushes worries about self-deception and rationalization back a step: *Everyone* believes he is in the right moral tribe, everyone thinks he punches for justice. Some of us are surely wrong about that, but when I believe myself in the right, how confident should I be that I am correct? Assessing whether my views are morally correct is a matter for moral philosophical investigation, but that is not my task here. Rather, I am interested in the process by which I take my own judgment to be of sufficient power to override the imperatives of civility. To decide my judgment warrants incivility, and indeed ennobles incivility as a special moral expression, requires confidence, and I want to know where that confidence comes from, what conditions may be giving rise to it. On that score, I think there is much besides believing oneself in the right or even being in the right that can feed confidence, that can tempt us to strongly favor uncivil expressions of our views over civil alternatives. Indeed, I often worry that our current social and political climate makes confidence about our incivilities all too easy.

A person engaging in critical righteous incivility will by definition act as an iconoclast. She departs from the status quo in favor of following her own moral judgment, breaking from prevailing norms to serve a good she takes as higher. This is a rather straightforward description of what critical righteous incivility entails, but our contemporary rhetoric often significantly enlarges upon these basics. We inhabit an age that depreciates conformity and abiding by conventional norms. Values such as standing apart from the crowd and thinking for oneself are generally prized. These values already and in their own right likely increase our receptivity to righteously uncivil tactics, but they are notably amplified in how we tend to describe incivility. We have many ready-to-hand ways to describe incivility in ways that render it not only acceptable but downright heroic.

The language in popular currency used to describe ostensibly admirable incivility often implies that the uncivil person is distinctively noble and uncommonly brave. The uncivil person "keeps it real," boldly saying what others dare not. He will deliver home truths no matter how little such truths please us, he will be "politically incorrect" and thus risk disapprobation. He will "speak truth to power" in bold defiance of what power can do. Identifying incivility with courage is also embedded in martial metaphorical language that implicitly likens the uncivil to warriors engaged in combat. The uncivil person performs figurative violence as he "owns," "spanks," "burns," or "roasts" his targets. He "takes the gloves off." In language evocative of dueling, he will "call out" others' flaws, hypocrisies, or errors, summoning them to own what they have said or done under open challenge. Even where limited disapproval of the uncivil is in play, our language can be martial. "Punching up"—directing one's incivility toward those who enjoy greater social privilege and power—is acceptable, while "punching down"—striking the more vulnerable—is not. This represents an ethos regarding our incivilities, but it is the ethos of martial contest and one that intensifies the bravery and nobility involved: When I punch up, I go after someone counted more formidable, more powerful, *bigger*, and presumably do so to favor the smaller among us.

Our culture's popular descriptions of incivility, I think, function to make it more appealing. They align incivility with rugged individualism, with heroism and strength, with nobility and courage. They invite the uncivil to see themselves as honorable warriors who welcome the perils of displeasing others without flinching. When I am uncivil, these descriptions provide a compelling story I can tell myself about what I do, a story that significantly increases confidence in my incivility by making it seem what a hero would do. And, not incidentally, we also have correspondingly unappealing stories I can tell myself about anyone who does not like it. For implicit in our alignment of incivility with strength and heroism is the suggestion that those who conform to civil norms or who dislike incivility are but frail and weak. This is most evident in what is surely our most storied way of identifying the uncivil person with a kind of violence.

Those we admire as critically and righteously uncivil are often praised as gadflies, but it is worth recalling what the metaphor entails. Actual gadflies startle the horses and cattle, their stings alarming herd animals primitively guided by dull habit and markedly sensitive to any disruption of the usual. The targets of the gadfly are creatures whose constitutional vulnerabilities require the protections herd behavior provides. Embedded in identifying the uncivil with the gadfly, then, is a contrast frequently invoked in defenses of the uncivil. Where incivility is aligned with strength, dislike of incivility or, worse, taking offense are associated with delicacy. The uncivil have the stuff to enjoy the rough and tumble of keeping it real, as well as a healthy disdain for the prim and prissy. Significantly, any wounds the uncivil deal others result from a strength differential: if those hurt by incivility would but toughen up, they would not be wounded. This too is embedded in some of our popular rhetoric regarding incivility and taking offense. Protesting harm done by incivility is sometimes dismissed as but testament to a weak constitution—it is but whining or mewling infantilism, the offended cast as delicate "snowflakes." Indeed, the "herd" is itself part of the idiom we can use to describe those who dislike our exercises in critical righteous incivility: Those who reject our nonconformity and noncompliance with civil norms do so because their dull, bovine nature requires it.

The trouble with our culturally commonplace ways of describing the uncivil and, by extension, those they would target is that they can infect how we think of our own incivilities. To engage in critical righteous incivility requires that I believe I am right in my judgments, and it requires confidence that uncivil expression is both warranted and good. It is on this latter point that our laudatory descriptions of incivility may invite trouble. Given our cultural rhetoric, the potential for valorizing self-deception is great: Lesser sorts may call me "rude" because I speak truth to power; they dislike my incivility because they are snowflakes. Lesser sorts think I "insult" because I just tell it like it is; they dislike it because they belong to the herd and can't handle the truth. We need only consult our own experiences to see the trouble here, for all of us, I suspect, have encountered confidently uncivil "heroes" we judge to wantonly offend out of juvenile hubris and misplaced estimations of their own nobility. When I am tempted to incivility I think righteous, I am often drawn up short by dread that I will become *that guy*.

One thing I notice about *that guy* when I encounter him is the perversity of his confidence. For all his purported love of the rough and tumble, he often does not face opposition and robust challenge to his views. This is not because his views are so clearly right, as he believes, but because others find it too distasteful to engage with him, his incivility rendering dialogue simply not worth the fractious, unpleasant trouble it would take. His high certainty in his own rightness and righteousness is thus maintained in a kind of epistemic naiveté, his confidence sustained in part because his views are far less tested and tried than those of others. This points to a broader concern about critical righteous incivility.

If I am going to be independent in thought and nonconformist in conduct, I want also to be *wise* in doing so. Being independently and unusually foolish is, after all, hardly a triumph. However, the chief mechanism for checking my own potential for foolishness is other people. Their displeasure, dissent, and disagreement can sound an alert that my views need refining, are incomplete or plainly wrong-headed. The more I am in thrall to heroic estimations of my righteous incivilities, the greater the worry that I effectively block this route to self-improvement, both by holding low opinions of others and by interacting in ways that, as a practical matter, will discourage challenge. When others do indeed know better than I, I will be far less likely to find that out. Incivility can thus place me at an epistemic disadvantage with respect to the rightness of my views. I may mistake aggressively guarding my views from challenge for having views that cannot be readily challenged. Put plainly, incivility may feed confidence by starving wisdom.

It is surely beneficial to be aware of cultural conditions that heroicize incivility, promote tribalism, and encourage hubris. Where, however, does this sort of analysis leave me with respect to my conduct and my temptations to incivility? What bearing, if any, ought broad cultural conditions have on how I think about my own incivilities? I am not ready to give up the notion that some incivilities *are* genuinely righteous. I am, however, forced to concede that I may not be especially good at picking these out, at resisting the myriad other forces in operation when I find incivility compelling and tempting. The culture works on me, influencing my broad attitudes and the judgments to which I will be prone. Recognizing this, a deeper problem emerges.

When I reflect on righteous incivility, as I have here, my reasoning about it must, out of necessity, be abstract. I seek to illuminate what *sorts* of reasons and motivations can keep incivility righteous. I look for ways to generalize and discover some broadly useful insights that might guide me through the particulars of experience. Yet precisely because such an endeavor requires generality and abstraction, it simplifies. It thus risks giving me an understanding of righteous incivility naively purified of the far messier forces that can be at work in me when I want to be uncivil. One of these forces is the culture's laudatory descriptions of incivility, but the wider challenge is just the gap between what I can settle in the armchair, in abstract reflection, and the tangled particulars of lived experience. There are myriad ways this gap can complicate our efforts at bringing moral conclusions to bear on life, but my interest is in how it registers in my own efforts to be civil and to keep the incivilities I allow myself righteous. On this score, my greatest trouble is that an abstract account of righteous incivility presents me with a person dramatically unlike myself. In simplifying into crisp abstraction what righteous incivility will look like, I also simplify the person who so acts. While I can imagine a person who circumspectly elects to operate from conscience and in pursuit of broad social-moral improvement, I doubt I can *be* that person. For I do not experience my own temptations to incivility in anything like the careful, reflective way the account describes.

Most basically, unlike those of my imagined righteously uncivil actor, my motivations are complex. The abstracted, conceptual account I can give of righteous incivility—appealing to its possible good effects or its connection to personal integrity—relies on a picture of human psychology that is rather spare. The account outlines cleanly defined moral reasons for acting uncivilly, but actual human motivation is murky, a mess and muddle of competing forces often understood best in retrospect, if we ever fully understand them at all. Worse still, while my motivations will *be* murky, I often experience them, in the moment, as clear: I will want to be uncivil and I will read this impulse as justified, noble, and right, purified of any complicating features I may later, in hindsight, discern. That I can experience a quick clarity that later dissolves under scrutiny makes me uncomfortably aware of a deeper challenge: The judgment calls I make about my impulses to incivility are typically made on the fly, quickly and in circumstances that are themselves rarely crisply defined or understood.

Most of my opportunities for incivility transpire in the course of a rather ordinary life. They occur as I encounter other people who speak in ways I find objectionable, avowing views I would dispute and, sometimes, views I abhor. Like most nowadays, my encounters with disagreement of this sort are both live and electronic, and I can deliver my incivilities both in person or in pixels. The latter sort do permit space for deliberation, but the pace of life is such that the judgment calls about civility I make most often transpire in some haste and in contexts I apprehend quickly rather than comprehensively. Because of this, my decisions to be uncivil often evince little of the reflective, ruminating quality of my more abstract reflections. What I believe in the armchair and what I do on the fly are sometimes embarrassingly, comically far apart. For evaluating situations in leisure and deciding what to do as circumstances arise are experientially quite different. What I do in the hustle and bustle of ordinary life will confess more about my dispositions than it will reflect conscious, considered choices. And, it turns out, many of my dispositions are far rattier than my leisurely reflections might indicate. This, in turn, makes much of my ruminating about how to *choose* well where temptations to incivility are concerned quite misleading.

In the flux and flow of ordinary life, my conduct leans heavily on dispositions I have developed over time, and these are far more central to my behavior than self-conscious decision-making. Factors such as my own life history, habits of mind and emotion, and patterns of behavior, as well as the social and cultural atmosphere I inhabit, will cumulatively structure the basic stuff of my experience. It is not simply that these will make me more disposed to some actions than others, but that how I read situations may be contoured in accord with my dispositions. They can inform how circumstances appear to me, what features of experience command my attention and what slip my notice, what I make of other people's speech or conduct, and of course, what behaviors register with me in any catalog of possible responses. Thus, by dint of contrasting dispositions born of variation in experience and habit, people can receive the same experience quite differently. Where one discerns insult, another may discern good fun; where one apprehends accord, another apprehends tension. Some, though surely not all, of these differences in interpreting a situation will owe to differences in developed disposition, and these differences will make a difference in how people behave. All of this will matter a great deal where I seek to be more civil and to better resist temptations to be otherwise.

Once I recognize that my behaviors, civil and uncivil alike, will be significantly steered by how experience, attitude, and habit have disposed me, it becomes far easier to see why dividing civility from ordinary good manners is so unsatisfying. Both civility and ordinary good manners appear to engage the same processes; both require interpreting situations and steering conduct to communicate respect, consideration, and toleration. Success in both will likewise often depend on developed disposition, on prior patterning that renders me more prone to one kind of response than another. This is in part why the early Confucian picture of the social behaviors that comprise civility and manners is so compelling: they recognize that efforts to be civil and polite profit best from working on dispositions, from cultivating an orientation toward others and toward shared social existence that renders incivility and rudeness less compelling. To be sure, their counsel does not resolve into any formula that would reliably divide truly righteous incivility from its lesser, ignoble kin. Rather, what they offer are ways to reduce the many dubious attractions incivility can have for me and ways to increase the appeal of civility. Indeed, I think the deep work on dispositions they offer ultimately transforms what the pull of righteous incivility will feel like. We will feel less of it, and when we do feel it, it will have a stronger prosocial character.

Before I turn to what the early Confucians can offer to address my temptations and inclinations to incivility, however, I need first to get a handle on why ordinary bad manners can be appealing. Like incivility, pedestrian bad manners can be quite attractive. However, just as our popular discourse treats political civility as distinct from having good manners, so too the reservations we express about manners differ from those we offer about civility. Because we align civility with shared public reasoning about deep values, we treat it as rather high-stakes business. Good manners, in contrast, are identified with our purportedly "private" conduct and the more mundane ways we conduct our social lives. Understanding why I sometimes *want* to be rude in ordinary, prosaic contexts is a crucial first step in wanting it less, so this is my focus in the next chapter.

Chapter 3

Temptations to Bad Manners

Before I began writing this chapter today, I had already been rude. I needed to purchase shoelaces and, it turns out, locating these in a typical grocery store is akin to seeking the proverbial needle in a haystack. My quick errand took time I did not wish to spare and so, having at long last found the laces, my impatience to get on with my day rendered me rude: I let the shop door slam in the face of a customer exiting just behind me, not even sparing a "Sorry!" over my shoulder as I did so. I thus begin work today having already failed at maintaining my resolve to be a more polite person. My expectation, however, is that you will forgive me this episode of rudeness and, moreover, will do so more readily than had I confessed to phoning my congressman to curse him for his political views.

Unlike political incivility, pedestrian bad manners appear not to involve dispute over deep social values. Instead, manners concern how we navigate the low-level, low-stakes, commonplace interactions of daily life. Where the temptations to political incivility invoke weighty concerns about moral conviction and principled breaches of social norms, the temptations to bad manners are far more modest. Indeed, *temptation* is an odd way to frame much of what transpires in the push-pull between ordinary politeness and ordinary rudeness.

When I let the door slam in the face of my fellow shopper, I was not tempted to it; I gave it no thought at all. I would not even have recognized what I had done were it not for the muffled and sarcastic "Thanks a lot!" I heard from the man now on the other side of the glass and left to push through on his own. It was only then that "temptation" really entered into my experience and I succumbed to a more conscious rudeness. Rather than apologizing, I silently protested, "Oh, please!" at this fellow begrudging me my haste. No need for him to inject his resentful objections, I thought; is it not obvious that I am in a *hurry*? Happily but embarrassingly, I did not, just then, follow this thought with what would come next: Having done with that unpleasant fellow who can surely open his own damn door, now I can get down to work on my book about good manners! But now that I am at last at my desk and ready to lay down pixels on laptop, I am obliged to exorcize the demon of considerable hypocrisy before beginning. At least, I console myself, I have a good example with which to begin, for I think that my morning's rudeness catches at much of the problem with ordinary good manners.

A typical day presents us with countless opportunities to be rude. Other people populate our experience in ways that make polite living an obstacle course. We pursue our purposes and projects, be these shoelace purchasing or book writing, while challenged to navigate coexistence with others who are likewise pursuing their own purposes and projects. Every interaction with others makes demands, even if the demand is sometimes that we leave someone else in peace. If I want to be polite, it can seem as if I am never off the clock, as if the *work* of courtesy is never-ending. In the company of others, there is always, it seems, something to *do*. This ubiquity suffices as partial explanation of why ordinary social politeness is so difficult.

Ordinary good manners require that we engage in conventional behaviors socially understood as signaling respect and consideration for others: We greet each other, beg pardon, take leave, say "please" and "thank you," and engage in myriad nonverbal gestures that symbolically function to acknowledge others. To get all this right requires attention, yet much will compete for that attention. Often we will fail in basic politeness not because we lack consideration or respect for others, but simply because we overlook them as we labor instead under our own preoccupations, aims, and desires. Attention is a kind of currency, and it is easily entirely spent just on managing our own needs. Moreover, the ubiquity of other people and thus the occasions calling for some attention can register as nickel-and-diming—it does not require much to exercise ordinary courtesies, but the accumulation of small charges on attention can nonetheless feel bankrupting. To be polite, then, entails getting good at managing an internal economy of attention.

Aware that I will be prone to rudeness where I let my own pre-occupations swamp my notice of others, I could of course simply resolve to better pay attention. The solution here is simple: Once I notice others, I can then make the requisite effort to display manners appropriate to how I encounter them. This strategy, however, is as unappealing as it is simple, and indirectly discloses additional challenges to being polite.

Most basically, human beings are not, it turns out, terribly adept at maintaining attention where they resolve to do so. For my own part, such resolutions do not make paying attention easier or more fluid, but instead increase the felt tax of paying attention: I must not only pay attention to others, I must pay attention to paying attention, assiduously keeping my resolve mentally present as I navigate the conditions and circumstances of daily life. This is not my own idiosyncratic weakness but a general feature of our cognitive lives. Edward Slingerland, who studies both Confucianism and the cognitive science of attention, explains that "cognitive control is a limited resource" and so, as he notes, the phrase "Pay attention!" is more than metaphorical.[1] Sustained efforts deplete, and the resources we have are finite. We may succeed, in one domain or for a time, but *paying* attention can indeed be bankrupting, ultimately demotivating improvement through exhaustion. Resolving to be more attentive to others, then, is not only unpleasant, it is unlikely to work.

The cognitive science concerning attention is not, for most of us, a direct element in how we consciously encounter the challenges of being polite. We do not, that is, have a formal, scientific understanding of our own limitations; we simply experience them. The science does, however, illuminate and explain why trying to be polite is so difficult and why failing is so easy. Noticing all that we need to notice in the mix and muddle of experience is, though, but a first obstacle among others. Even if we can direct our attention as we should, we may yet fail. Attention alone does not suffice to make us polite. This is evident already in my rudeness of this morning.

My letting the door slam in someone's face was a failure of attention, but my declining to apologize cannot be so explained. My fellow shopper's sarcastic gratitude did summon my attention and, once attending, I opted to be rude, to carry on just as I had carried on, as if he did not exist. This is a different style of rudeness, then. It is consciously practiced and deliberately inflicted. And, regrettably, it too is commonplace, even as its internal mechanics are different. While paying attention can be tiring, steering conduct toward politeness can be tiresome. Ordinary politeness involves undertaking myriad small gestures that can, in the sum of human concerns, seem trivial and thus quite irritating. Polite gestures not only deplete, they can seem to deplete rather pointlessly, our efforts directed toward performances of "respect" or "consideration" that are as fussy as they are meaningless. These are indeed *tempting* thoughts and, significantly, they can work on us at two levels.

In declining to apologize to my fellow shopper this morning, I opted not to be polite in a discrete circumstance, to receive his complaint as a petty demand I would answer by pettily and deliberately ignoring him. I admit that I am often tempted to rudeness in just this way, even when not explicitly challenged by another. Typically, these temptations arise while I am in thrall to preoccupations I judge more significant or that simply weigh on me more. In the balance of things I need or ought to do, being polite simply does not rate as terribly significant relative to the rest of my conduct. Put most plainly, I can and do sometimes tell myself that being polite really *does not matter*, or, at the least, it matters far less than the rest of what I am presently doing or pursuing. Sometimes of course we are justified in concluding that politeness should yield before other concerns: Interruption is generally rude, but if your house is on fire, it would be right to interrupt your telephone call to tell you so. The trouble is that we can readily overestimate the importance of competing claims on our conduct, effectively multiplying house fires. This tendency may arise from rank self-absorption, but it can also have less damningly selfish sources. Perhaps pressures of life simply accumulate—we can, after all, be burdened by concerns and responsibilities genuinely profound and compelling—and being polite simply registers as inconsequential in comparison. So we incline against polite conduct, not bothering with small niceties and privileging instead whatever, at the moment, seems to matter more. A greater worry is that the temptation to count displays of politeness trivial reaches beyond discrete moments.

I can more easily manage being polite in particular circumstances if I am generally motivated and disposed to be a polite person. I will be more well-mannered if I have reliable practices of attention and conduct, if I develop behavioral and speech routines that I can enact through habit. That is, I will have a better chance of being polite in discrete circumstances if I have a rather global commitment to trying to be a *polite person* and have, toward this end, cultivated sound habits in my interactions with others. This too, however, is a kind of work and, like any habit acquisition, will require steady effort and, more foundationally, a belief that the result of my labor will be worth it. Doubts about just this, about the worth of lending finite energies to cultivating good manners as part of one's behavioral makeup, are,

I suspect, one of most substantial temptations we face. Such doubts include worries about triviality, for just as we can discount the significance of good manners in a particular instance, so too we can discount them in the wider framework of a life. Indeed, the impulse to discount good manners is stronger here: Of all the ways I may wish to work on myself and direct effort toward self-improvement, being habitually polite is hardly the stuff of high and noble aspiration. Relative to other ways I may improve myself through devoted effort and determination, it seems of small account. Worse still, being the sort of person who devotes considerable effort to cultivating good manners can itself seem deeply unattractive.

Concerns about triviality are, at root, about far more than whether having good manners matters in the scope of human concerns. The sense that good manners are of little account rides on our sense of what practicing good manners entails, of what being well-mannered requires of us. To become a polite person entails not just work, but work we may well worry distorts character rather than improving it. On this score, the reservations about the worth of good manners are many. Judith Martin, known to many by her column name, Miss Manners, ably summarizes the most core complaints about politeness: "It's artificial! It's arbitrary! It's stuffy! It's prudish! It represses people from expressing their true feeling! It inhibits little children! It's hypocritical! It's dishonest! And—*it uses forks!*"[2] For me at least, these more elaborate complaints ground my temptation to see good manners as trivial. There is some truth in all of these complaints and they highlight the ways in which being polite can register as voluntary self-"improvement" undertaken for no higher end than being socially pleasing to others. In being polite, I will hide what I feel, abide by capricious rules I can in no way justify, simulate attitudes I do not endorse, behave decorously rather than naturally, and, most generally, align my conduct with social norms that too often seem but anxious, arbitrary micromanaging. The concerns here echo, in broadest form, those attached to civility: Wanting to be polite is attached to thinking this will make me a *better* person, but aspects of practicing politeness cast doubt on whether being polite would indeed be better.

Martin's list of complaints against ordinary good manners contains much, but out of all these complaints, what most registers with me are a couple of wider worries that capture them all: practicing good manners involves much fakery, and there is something deeply joyless about good manners. Good manners are dishonest and, worse still, they are not even fun about it. These wider worries feature both in historical criticisms of manners and in more contemporary complaints, so it is worth dwelling on the temptation they represent.

Just as uncivil people sometimes do, impolite people sometimes explain their conduct by claiming to be "keeping it real." They thereby profess their rejection of the dissembling and dissimulation manners require, and, more ambitiously, catch at the apparent hypocrisy, dishonesty, and artificiality of good manners. This is, moreover, no new development in thinking critically about manners but has long reach in Western cultural history. Socrates is perhaps the first Western cultural hero to keep things real, avowing that he would not speak as others do but instead speak plainly and directly (which, it turned out, sometimes involved communicating his disrespect for others).[3] Some of the most vivid depictions of the fakery entailed in manners are, however, of more recent vintage. One cannot read Edith Wharton's novels without thinking that the people who populate her narratives suffer, both individually and collectively, from a manners culture that renders human interaction akin to a forced march through a funhouse of distorting mirrors. Each is to each deformed by repressive behavioral strictures; none are known by, or knowable to others, for all are concealed beneath a dense artifice of etiquette. Manners render them *unreal*—that is, phony. This is a problem perhaps best philosophically represented by Jean-Jacques Rousseau.

Rousseau's writing on the distortions of good manners, on the unrealness they impose, likens manners to a "uniform and deceitful veil," a mask that renders all alike and produces interaction corrupted by insincerity and falsity. Polite society, Rousseau protested, is not simply deceptive, but also actively stifles individuality in favor of bovine conventionality: One must follow custom, "but never one's own genius," acting always within the circumscribed constraints of "that herd called society."[4] And, with all effectively masked in manners, human beings lose the "ease of seeing through one another," allowing vice to flourish because we can never really tell what anyone is about.[5] This is strong stuff, but it catches at problems both practical and profound in practicing good manners. The fakery in play is not just that I will speak or behave insincerely in some social setting, but is shot all through our epistemic lives and existential self-understanding, at whether we can know others or can even know ourselves.

Rousseau's objection comprehends a familiar social experience: We spend time talking with others, ostensibly communicating, yet can nonetheless come away entirely uncertain of their views, values, attitudes, or, most broadly, who they *really* are. The pleasantry imposed by good manners may not always stifle "genius," but it may yet deny us the ability to know others as we would wish, to know them beyond the blandly conventional social face they present. We implicitly appeal to something like this concern when we suggest that good manners are less necessary between friends. Friendship, we judge, entails greater freedom and transparency in communication. Friends need less concealment and dissembling, and this speaks well of friendship and is part of what we especially prize about it. Manners can enforce a banal and opaque sameness, but really knowing others profits from seeing the idiosyncratic, the personal, and, most basically, the person being straightforwardly herself. If we want to form meaningful bonds with others, we want to *know* them, and good manners can seem to inhibit our ability to do just this. This concern notably reflects an optimism about others, about how knowing them well may afford increase in interest, affection, and attachment, but there are also potently cynical reasons for wanting to see behind the mannerly mask.

A long-standing complaint about the fakery of manners, evident in Rousseau's claim about vice, is that manners can assist us in misleading and manipulating others. In broad strokes, one can be pleasing to others precisely because it is advantageous to rank self-interest. The forms of this general complaint are varied. One pernicious historical version frets that the "lower orders" can use good manners to simulate membership in a class to which they do not properly belong. We have largely abandoned inflexible class-consciousness, yet we retain an updated form of this worry in the suspicion that good manners enable apple polishing, social climbing, and power seeking. The opacity afforded by conformity to good manners can be cunningly turned toward pleasing one's superiors, impressing those from whom one seeks favor, or flattering the powerful. Here too, the complaint is that manners involve the presentation of a facade, with surface appearance artfully arranged. In the cynical worry, however, the inability to know others disables our defenses against manipulation, to know where we really stand with others and how we register as useful to their self-interest. In short, good manners can hide foul rot. It is this that provoked Samuel Johnson to read Lord Chesterfield's storied instructions regarding good manners and lament that "they teach the morals of a whore, and the manners of a dancing-master."[6] Johnson's protest registers the reality that sometimes the people with the "best manners" are also the most calculating, their pleasing appearance a seduction we should resist. And it likewise registers the suspicion that devoting oneself to cultivating good manners is a project that cheapens the one who undertakes it.

Johnson's biting critique of Chesterfield emerges from a cynicism deeper than mere worries about manipulation of others and invokes the way that cultivating manners can distort the well-mannered person. This is implicit in Rousseau's work as well. Manners do not just work on others, they work on the practitioner herself and may deform her character. In being pleasing to others, we can become pleased with ourselves, embracing the superficial social signaling that wins others' approval as a signal that we are all we ought to be. This can be both a moral and an existential problem. We can mistake conventional social gestures that convey an appearance of virtue for virtue itself, developing a pride in looking good that obscures failures to be good. Existentially, as Rousseau suggests, we can so fully take on board social estimations of how we ought to be and appear that we fail to query our own "genius"—that is, to investigate what we judge to be *really* worthwhile, important, and valuable to ourselves. In both cases, conformity to external and markedly superficial standards risks stunting our finer possibilities. Fakery can be totalizing, for it may root into the self-conception of the mannerly practitioner, seducing her into "bovine" self-satisfaction. Tightly tethered to the herd, she contentedly avoids the free and open spaces of her own rich individuality or the hard and arduous work of developing robust, deep virtue.

Taken together, these many complaints about the fakery of good manners can suggest a deeply dystopian picture. Reliance on good manners alienates us from ourselves, encourages manipulation through superficial pleasantry, and enforces distance that inhibits close, knowing human relationships. Perversely, these unhappy outcomes clarify a deeper aspect of the triviality of good manners. It is not that good manners do not matter; it is that good manners do not matter to what *really matters*. The rich value in knowing others, both the good and the ill, and the profound good of knowing myself are lost where our efforts too devotedly skim along the surface of mere appearances and bland conformity. This kind of "not mattering" does indeed matter if what we want are lives that encourage what is most robust and fine in our relations and in ourselves.

The uncertainty about others and alienation from oneself imposed by the strictures of manners goes some distance toward explaining why good manners are often perceived as rather joyless. Writers such as Wharton sketch an unhappy world of people keeping "good company" regulated by manners, but the salient sense of "good" here has nothing of ease, enjoyment, pleasure, or delight. It is all bland sterility, dull decency, and empty artful formality. It is, put plainly, *no fun*. There is of course much in life that is worthwhile that is not fun, but at their worst, good manners can seem a rather puritanical enemy of fun. Indeed, practicing good manners may not just incidentally cut off routes to joy, but may more actively treat joy as the path to perdition. This is both because good manners can involve forms of direct self-regulation that inhibit enjoyment and because a general disposition to good manners can operate like a disposition against enjoyment.

Practicing good manners involves all sorts of self-regulation, ways we restrain and steer conduct in accord with the conventional behavioral rules attached to being polite. These rules do tend to shift with the times—what one era counts impolite, a later era may permit—but the rules always involve restraints upon conduct that inhibit ease and encourage self-monitoring. By itself, the imposed watchfulness required for good manners can inhibit enjoyment, but it bears emphasizing that etiquette, the rules for good manners, often includes rules explicitly discouraging fun. My favorite example of this is historical: Lord Chesterfield's condemnation of laughter. Laughter, he avers, is "low and unbecoming," typically aroused by "low buffoonery."[7] Then there is "the disagreeable noise it makes, and the shocking distortion of the face that it occasions." Chesterfield offers himself as a role model, smugly noting, "[I] am as willing and as apt to be pleased as anybody; but I am sure that since I have had the full use of my reason, nobody has ever heard me laugh."

While Chesterfield's counsel against laughter represents an extreme form of self-management, it is of a piece with a broader logic: good manners require tight control. And tight control, in turn, entails forfeiting certain pleasures. If one is to be well-mannered, after all, one must "*sacrifice to the graces.*"[8] We have mercifully abandoned any generalized prohibition on laughter, but good manners still, and always, will require that one cannot laugh every time one would wish. More generally, being polite entails countless tiny sacrifices to the graces, and, once we have sacrificed enough, we may well worry that we have disabled our capacities for joy. We do not simply have less of joy, we become joyless people. This worry is humorously captured in an inquiry Judith Martin, in her capacity as "Miss Manners," received. "Have you ever," her interlocutor implored:

1. eaten a pizza with bare fingers?
2. been to a bowling alley (of your own free will)?
3. drank a six-pack of beer?
4. called a man a "hunk"?
5. ever not worn underwear on a hot day?
6. eaten fried chicken straight from the bucket?
7. ever gone on a date in a pickup truck?
8. kept wearing tennis shoes with holes in them, just because they were comfortable?[9]

The detailed urgency of this list, I confess, resonates deeply with my own temptations to discount the worth and importance of good manners. Surely, as the writer implies, it is *important* to human well-being to some-times eat from paper cartons, forgo "proper" attire, and, most basically, follow one's natural promptings wherever they indecorously lead.[10]

The deeper worries evinced by Martin's interlocutor concern aspects of life that we prize, aspects such as relaxation, spontaneity, and disinhibition. These are not what we might typically include in a list of life's highest values, but a life bereft of them would be poorer indeed. Worse yet would be a life lived in such a way that we deliberately sacrifice our capacity to recognize their value, becoming people who not only don't have fun, but *can't*. The concern that manners are an enemy of joy, at its worst, may amount to the concern that devotion to politeness will make *me* an enemy of joy, a person who stridently condemns, in herself and in others, impulses that give life much of its flavor and delight. (Or the kind of person who *boasts* of never laughing!) This, to be sure, is why people committed to good manners are often represented as rather schoolmarmish, scolds who refuse to recognize that a fine and rich life can profit from some behavioral slack and slouching. Indeed, I think the specter of the schoolmarm indirectly indicates an additional way that being bad mannered is fun.

At risk of confessing too much about my own temperament, I must admit that one strong appeal of bad manners is that being naughty is itself often attractive and deeply enjoyable. In addition to the enjoyment that relaxation, spontaneity, and disinhibition bring in their own right, availing myself of these at the wrong moments is itself a kind of temptation. Such is to say that the trouble with schoolmarms is that they can, rather against their will, *invite* spitballs. Indeed, spitballs are all the more fun when one can shoot them in oppositional defiance, under forces that would insist you hold fire. This too is a kind of joy that an emphasis on being polite seems to miss, even as it may increase our temptations to seek it. The dynamic in play here is one best represented by early Chinese philosophers, known as Daoists, who opposed the Confucians. Contemporary commentator Joel Kupperman phrases the principle, which he calls "Laozi's Law," most directly: "The consequences of pushing for something often will include elements that amount to the opposite of what is pushed for."[11] As Kupperman wryly observes, the surest way to get a group of toddlers to put carrots up their noses is to announce, "Do not put carrots up your noses."[12]

Injunctions to be polite, to cultivate good manners, can often register as the kind of *pushes* Kupperman describes. What would, absent the push, not necessarily seem all that attractive can swell in its appeal precisely because it is forbidden. Transgression can be fun, things we are told not to do made all the more interesting precisely because we are told not to do them. This is the subtext in the list of "naughtiness" Martin's interlocutor catalogs. He doubts not simply her capacity for lower delights, but her ability to reap pleasure from occasional transgressive conduct, to break her own standards for a bit of fun. Martin, he implies, not only fails to appreciate these joys, her push for good manners perversely increases their appeal for others.

The triviality, fakery, and anhedonic aspects of good manners, taken together, constitute powerful reasons to doubt the worth of good manners. Sometimes reasons such as these will tempt me to be rude. Indeed, my declining to apologize to my fellow shopper is an example of succumbing. However, the real pinch of these reasons is that they also constitute a more global and formidable inducement: the temptation not to care, or not to care overmuch, about making good manners part of my reliable behavior patterns. Succumbing to this temptation, it is important to note, need not entail being willfully and consistently rude. Rather, it simply entails not *trying* to be polite, not making the rules of manners my steady standard for behavior but instead behaving well-mannered or ill-mannered, as I will and as the spirit moves me. It entails most of us being just as we presently are: sometimes attentive and respectful, sometimes not; sometimes openly rude, sometimes not; sometimes socially pleasant and considerate, sometimes not; sometimes crude and cutting, sometimes not. In short, the temptation is to see manners as a bother not worth any special effort or attention.

As is the case with my temptations to incivility, when I catalog the doubts I have about the worth of manners, I can almost persuade myself that improving my manners is not worth it. Here too, however, worries about self-deception attach and I am forced to wonder if I am more than a little self-serving in my complaints about manners. Most basically, even as I appeal to formidable historical critics and observers of manners—folk like Wharton, Rousseau, and Johnson—I must acknowledge that times have changed. My daily experience is not at all close kin to a Wharton novel of stifling and hypocritical social intercourse. Indeed, to identify the comparably mild strictures of contemporary etiquette with Wharton's world would require much unseemly and melodramatic overstatement. Our standards for good manners are far more permissive, our culture far more awash in honesty and blunt talk, and our latitude to be ourselves far greater than Wharton, or any of these authors, would likely have imagined possible. I can still of course protest that manners require fakery and conformity, but it does not do to overstate the case, to indulge in overwrought claims about etiquette "stifling" what Rousseau would call my "genius." Much more troubling than this, however, is a second worry about self-deception.

While there can be principled reasons for skepticism about the worth of good manners, my doubts tend not to have the consistency principle would demand. Rather, my attitudes toward manners vary with circumstances, and vary in discomfiting ways. I most often doubt the worth of manners when I wish to be rude or to excuse myself for having been rude. I rarely suffer such doubts when another has been rude to me. Indeed, when I am on the receiving end of rudeness, I am far more likely to profess the importance of manners and lament their general decline. In this, I am not alone. I have on occasion asked my students to bring in examples of rudeness, and

although I encourage them to select examples from their own conduct, most do not. Instead, they bring in cases of having suffered
under the rudeness of others. More startling still, their examples are
commonly colored with the indignation and high dudgeon more
typically associated with us older sorts. I suspect many of us are like
this, ready to discount or fail to notice our own poor manners, but
prey to outrage when treated rudely. Like incivility, impoliteness is
most appealing when it is mine; when it is yours, it is, plainly and
obviously, just awful.

Variations in our responses to rudeness, what we will excuse and
what will ground affront, indicate that doubts about the worth of
manners can be quite self-serving. Even worse, we can be remark-
ably disingenuous in our more particular complaints. Bad manners
seem far less trivial when they are directed at me, and I find the same
is true of my students. The cases of rudeness they typically raise are
striking in their modesty: being interrupted, having someone cut in
line, failures to say "please" or "thank you," and, yes, people letting
doors slam in their faces. Moreover, when they express outrage at
these minor slights and snubs, their rhetoric locates deep affront in
small gestures. They will protest: "It was as if I didn't exist!" or "She
behaved as if I didn't matter at all!" or "You'd think I was his servant!"
My suspicion is that this rhetoric indicates much about what good
manners *do* and *are for*, but it suffices here to note that we seem far
less tempted to count manners trivial if we are the ones who feel dis-
respected, ignored, or treated inconsiderately. Our protestations that
manners are meaningless, fussy, and unimportant begins to look like
self-serving rationalization.

Putting aside these observations about how we can be self-
serving in our skepticism about manners, I have to wonder just what
not trying to be polite would actually look like. It is rather easy to
long for a world of robust laughter, spontaneous enjoyments, and
people who are appealing in their realness, a world in which social

climbing, puling flattery, and insincerity are exiled. But this is not the world we are likely to win by slacking with our manners. If one worry about good manners is that they enable social climbing, power seeking, and manipulation, I suspect that permitting slack in our manners will not change things. Indeed, it is likely to make them worse.

If I permit myself to be polite or impolite just as my impulses in a given situation dictate, I cynically expect that the results will be rather unattractive. Most of us, I hazard, will feel the polite impulse as we engage with people who enjoy some power in the world. In contrast, we will be most willing to let ourselves go and be "real" with those who enjoy less power. Even people who might openly sneer at polite convention are likely to be courteous to those whose good favor they seek or wish to preserve. This explains, after all, why human beings more reliably enact courtesy with their bosses than with store clerks, waitstaff, or housekeepers. If we permit slack in our attention to manners, our moments of slack will not distribute evenly across the population of those we encounter, but will permit more open expression of pernicious and often unconscious biases we have about social status. In other words, pity the poor and low-status for all the "realness" abandoning manners will deal them. This, more than all other concerns, operates for me as a check on my willingness to discount the worth of manners. And, as with my temptations to incivility, the issue is one of self-distrust.

As I address more fully later in this book, we have good reasons to think that abandoning good manners, of failing to *try* to be polite, will magnify many social ills and inequalities. We inhabit a social world that steers us, in ways both subtle and unsubtle, to treat people differently based on status arrangements that are too often inequitable. The mechanics of this are complex and often unconscious, but may here be reduced to the plain worry that if I operate on my impulses, those impulses will reflect the social inequalities in which they have developed. In my own case, I can most easily recognize this in my employment experiences.

I am treated considerably better now that I am a professor than I was when I worked as a maid. It is not that in shifting occupations, I have shifted into more polite company. It is that my social status changed and, along with it, others' responses to me changed. Those I encountered in both occupations were the usual range of people— some nicer, some not; some pleasant, some unpleasant. Yet when I was a maid, people apparently felt less pressure or inner compulsion to mind their manners: I was more frequently treated with disrespect and inconsideration. My housekeeping clients were generally not trying to be rude, they simply were not trying to be polite and my status as their maid did not trigger their impulses to show respect. My being a professor does trigger those impulses in others, or at least more so than it does for maids, so I now enjoy more of the courtesies from others than I once did. I do not think my experiences in this regard are unique or distinctive. Indeed, the worry I express here is that I am indistinguishable from those I encountered in my housekeeping work: I am likely to be more polite where social status arrangements operate to make me so and less likely to be polite where they do not. To put it bluntly, so long as I just follow whatever impulses arise in me, I distrust myself to treat housekeepers as courteously as I will professors. And I adamantly do not approve of that in myself. I do not wish to be this way, but neither can I discount the likelihood that, ungoverned by a commitment to manners, I will be. If part of my doubt about the worth of manners is a desire to "keep it real," I best start by being real with myself. Like the allure of incivility, the temptations to bad manners can have me acting in ways that exacerbate social ills I otherwise deplore. Indeed, this is one good reason I cannot well credit our contemporary habit of considering good manners distinct from civility. Lacking either can leave the people we encounter, and maybe even the world entire, worse off, and it really is not clear I can well have one but not the other. This is why, for the rest of the book, I will follow the Confucians and treat civility and manners together.

Having dived into my temptations toward incivility and ordinary rudeness, I am left with a sense that the temptations, while sometimes powerful, are coupled with doubts. I cannot quite convince myself that these temptations are typically well grounded, uncluttered by low motives, hypocrisy, or self-deception. By itself, assaying the mixed nature of these temptations goes some distance toward resisting them, but a focus on temptation is itself somewhat unsatisfying, for it does not yet well motivate me to the work of being better. I may know more about why succumbing to incivility and rudeness is bad, but what would most profit my motivation is understanding why civility and politeness are good. This is why I find the early Confucian philosophers so useful: for them, cultivating good manners is about pursuing and preserving profound goods, goods we cannot well win without manners. So let me leave temptation behind and imagine this good.

Chapter 4

The Big Values

The British philosopher Philippa Foot once scoffed about good manners that "one could hardly be devoted to behaving *comme il faut*," to being polite, but she clearly had not read the Confucians.[1] Of philosophers, historically and globally, there are none who compare to the Confucians for a passionate commitment to manners and civility. Some of their passion is surely rooted in social, cultural, and political realities long past. The practices of *li*—the singular concept through which the Confucians expressed what we divide into civility, manners, and etiquette—were indubitably woven into long-standing traditions within monarchial court culture and elaborate lineage kinship systems. Yet despite the vast cultural gaps between the Confucians and ourselves, much of what they offer has an abiding appeal. For me, this appeal owes most to how well the two Confucians who are my focus—Confucius and Xunzi—capture aspects of life we hold valuable even as we often fail to notice them. But the aspects of life the Confucians emphasize have little to do with how we most often represent civility and manners in a contemporary idiom, and the contrast is an instructive point of entry to their passion.

Much of my own struggle against temptations to be rude or uncivil has to do with chafing at disagreeable duty. I have a guilty awareness that I ought not say whatever I think or bluntly pursue my own ends indifferent to other people, and this awareness is coupled with an irritable desire just to speak as I find and do my own thing, as I will. At its worst, under all this temptation and irritability lurks a restive impatience with the ostensibly big values that manners and civility recommend. In our standard contemporary understandings of civility and good manners, tolerance and respect are key. In summary form, I need to be tolerant of others because this is what coexistence in a pluralistic society requires. As Clifford Orwin explains, civility works as "a bond uniting honest men busy minding their own affairs," each free to pursue what he values without treading on others' ability to do the same.[2] Respect similarly works to signal that we see others' independence. I need to show respect because people are not things to be treated any way we please, and good manners implicitly acknowledge that other people are not objects for our use, not ours to summarily direct, command, or control. Thus, as Sarah Buss explains, when we say, "Pass the salt, please," the symbolic content of the request, the message embedded in our convention, is "Pass the salt, you are worthy of respect."[3] Since you are a person, not a thing, I must *ask*, not order, you to do as I wish.

Being civil and polite, in these understandings, is principally about not doing damage, not undermining a free society of plural values and not violating the self-worth of individuals doing their own thing just as I do mine. Good manners, this tempts me sometimes to think, is but a tax we pay in order to coexist, and thus, like actual taxes, paying it is a necessary but irksome duty. When I think of manners this way, I incline to agree with Philippa Foot: I cannot be devoted to *that*. I can comply, but it will often feel forced and entail unhappy exercises of will to do so. The Confucian program of manners and civility has for me an entirely different atmospheric. It may not inspire passionate devotion, but it makes me *care* about manners and civility in ways our standard contemporary accounts cannot.

Being polite and civil does, to be sure, guard against doing harm, but this, the Confucians encourage me to recognize, is a stingy way to represent *all* it does. Respect and toleration are valuable not simply to avoid harm, but because they enable us to fulfill a fundamental aspect of ourselves: our need and desire for other people. I am not simply an individual with her own values and views, purposes, and projects, I am a social creature, one who depends on others in ways both banal and profound. The most ambitious promise of a Confucian approach to manners rests in its amplifying my attention to what being a social creature entails and honoring how very much, for me, living well means living well *with others*. The Confucians thus articulate a case for manners that hooks into big values that I do not have to *try* to want or prize. I already and without special schooling in the "proper" moral attitude want to have friends and companions I love and enjoy, a community in which I can robustly belong, and, most broadly of all, a sense of well-being with and among other human beings. These are such native and natural desires that they come effortlessly. To be sure, I do sometimes despair of other people and feel the pull of misanthropic impulses, but I do not *wish* to feel this—indeed, wanting to feel otherwise is an indelible part of such feelings. The Confucian case for manners and civility is hooked to all of this: to the need and desire for connection with others, and to the despair and disappointment of not being so connected. Where motivation is concerned, this difference in emphasis makes a significant difference.

It is pragmatically useful to have civil norms that act as collective safeguards of our individual independence: We need to coexist, but we also need the freedom to disagree and to set our own courses in our individual lives. In the broad social and political scheme of things, this is indeed prudent and sensible. But I do not live in the broad social and political scheme of things. I live with other people— friends, kin, neighbors, coworkers, and strangers at grocery stores. The abstractions of a pluralistic society and autonomous individuals who warrant respect as people fail to connect well with the life I in fact have. My relations with actual others careen from high blessing to perceived curse, from warm fellow feeling to abject alienation. They just refuse to stay put the way abstract generalities will. The pull of manners is, for the Confucians, experienced in just this, in wanting more of what is good and sustaining in our relations with others and less of what is alienating and damaging. The closest analogue to this orientation in contemporary work on manners appears in the myriad advice columns penned by etiquette writers.

The inquiries etiquette columnists typically receive are far less about what formal etiquette rules would dictate than about how to manage interpersonal relations in ways that render them more fruitful or less alienating—it is relatively rare that the rules themselves are unclear or puzzling. Instead, people struggle with the emotional and relational aspects of dealing with others. People do not want to know how to respect those with whom they disagree—that bloodlessly abstract formulation—they want to know how to speak with Uncle Frank over Thanksgiving dinner when he obnoxiously opines about politics. And their interest is not in getting this right in accordance with a broad social and political commitment to pluralism, they long instead for ways to navigate sometimes fractious, sometimes disappointing, but personally significant relations with the people in their lives. They want to enjoy Thanksgiving dinner and struggle with how terribly hard this often is. It is hard to know what to do or say, and it can even be hard to keep trying. Yet our sociality positions us to care, to celebrate relations that sustain us and regret when they do not. This, for the Confucians, is why manners are so important. Their passionate devotion to manners is, at root, a passionate devotion to our relations with other people, an awareness that it is neither good nor desirable to separate thriving as individuals from thriving with others. We live, in ways both basic and profound, in dependency on other people. Motivation to practice good manners will find increase the more we appreciate the depth and reach of this dependency.

In its most basic form, our sociality is evident in the myriad necessary and prudent dependencies that ground any ordinary life and its activities. Satisfying our most basic needs relies upon systems of cooperation developed over generations of human history. That I can type these words in the early morning hours depends upon uncountable others: those who devised and maintained the electrical grid providing light and powering my laptop; those who educated me, teaching me everything from grammar to typing to philosophy; those who built the chair on which I sit and those who developed the woodworking techniques upon which chair-building depends; those who designed my laptop's technology, those who assembled it; those who created written language that can capture thought in forms less ephemeral than speech. I could go on, but suffice it to say that representing what is presently transpiring *merely* as my solitary activity, as "Amy writing a book," obscures how foundationally dependent this activity and my pursuit of it relies on others. Thinking in this way quickly renders clear that it is not only in our ambitious and heroic activity that we "stand on the shoulders of giants." If you are sitting in a chair reading this, you are sitting on the shoulders of giants. The most basic aspects of our material existence are afforded us only because we have others, and what I individually do, and can do, rests and relies on what many others do.

Once we take measure of how radically even our most basic life activities depend upon vast histories and systems of collective human effort, we can readily recognize the importance of effective strategies for maintaining this effort, for sustaining our abilities to work collectively and cooperatively. In this most rudimentary sense, then, we can understand the practices of manners as one such strategy. Because we do need each other, we likewise need ways to keep the social bonds necessary for cooperation intact. Our good manners and civil practices can be understood as mechanisms for signaling sociality and dependency. That I am respectful and tolerant is far less about acknowledging our separation as individuals distinct from each other than about acknowledging the ways we are connected and need each other. We rely upon social cooperation in order to ground our well-being, and our social cooperation in turn relies upon our ability to get along, whether that takes the shape of sharing resources, working together, or navigating difference. This way of understanding our dependency is a start at what the Confucians are after in their passion for manners, but, crucially, it is only a start, and a rudimentary one at that.

It is important that we acknowledge the many brute and basic ways we need each other, but there is also something rather trans-actional in this understanding. To be sure, facilitating cooperation pitched at fulfilling our needs is something, but it can be a rather stingy something where motivating manners is concerned. It might make me hold my tongue and politely put up with you because needs must, but it does not yet approach the stuff of passion we see in the Confucians.

Both Confucius and Xunzi ultimately conceive our mannerly practices as expressions of that which is finest and most exquisitely, nobly human. Xunzi describes li—manners and civility—as a "means of nuture."[4] He likens its effect to the way that exquisite music "nurtures" the ear and fine flavors "nurture" the palate. As these comparisons suggest, manners address needs, but do so in a fashion that elevates and exalts. We must eat, but when we eat finely prepared food, the act of dining is transformed—appetite begins in brute physical necessity but becomes ornamented, rich, and pleasing experience. So too with manners. We need to cooperate in order to survive, but manners promise to transform cooperation into something both more substantive and more meaningful than transactional need fulfillment. I can fulfill my biological need for nourishment by eating a messy sandwich over the sink alone, but life would be poorer if this were all I could ever do. Dining at table with finely prepared food better nurtures my well-being, well-being that includes notably more than not being hungry. So too, transactionally civil interactions *could* plausibly work to sustain coexistence, but were this all we could expect, it would be spare and mean, failing to nurture the finer and more deeply satisfying aspects human interaction can yield. In their most robust version, then, good manners are meant to express what is rich and fine in our shared humanity. Indeed, for the Confucians, maintaining our social bonds with others is what renders us fully, magnificently *human*. We all are, in a trivial biological sense, human, but to be a human being, in a morally and existentially significant sense, is to be a human being in relation with other human beings. This fuller sense of our humanity can be made evident if we consider just how it comes about and what it would mean to lose it.

When we consider the ways that human beings are social, we can discern our dependencies on cooperative activities and structures, but, significantly, we begin to depend on others long before we ourselves are capable of cooperation. We are born into the world as bundles of need, infants reliant on the caretaking of others for survival. In their caretaking, parents, grandparents, and siblings ensure our survival, but notably do so in the absence of reciprocity. The infant gives little back, a reality perhaps best captured not in Confucian sources but in a satirical article from *The Onion* titled "Area Baby Doesn't Have Any Friends."[5] The baby, *The Onion* observes, "often alienates those outside of his family circle," for he falls asleep in the presence of others, evinces no interest in their cares or conversation, bursts into "crying fits" regardless of what others are doing, and produces foul odors. Babies, let's face it, are ill-mannered, narcissistic louts. It is only through much nurturing and care that they develop the social-emotional capacities and competencies to form relationships with others, and these capacities and competencies come to them through the arduous efforts others, first by the efforts of family and then by wider circles of community. This sensibility informs the Confucians' long-storied commitment to family, but it also grounds their commitment to manners.

None of us begin with "friends" in the world, with relationships that we develop in reciprocity and mutual care, but the Confucian account of manners comprehends a great moral beauty in the way that the efforts of giving others effectively give us ourselves, transforming us into persons who can form rich, meaningful relations with others. Much of our early learning is learning sociality, as we come to recognize others as persons with their own needs, desires, feelings, and experiences. Much of how this is accomplished is through learned good manners: the "area baby" will have a shot at friendship as he acquires habits in listening when others speak, attending to interpersonal dynamics, reciprocating appropriate emotions, and when he is commanded by more than his own immediate feelings. And it will largely be the everyday manners of his kin and caretakers that will school him in all of this. We are born human, we might say, but we are given our *humanity* by and with others. Under their tuition and care, we learn how to form bonds with others, bonds that in turn importantly foster our well-being. This presentation of our dependency, then, reaches far beyond the rudimentary need for cooperation and emphasizes instead the way much of what we prize in life—friendship, love, companionship—is fashioned from learned sociality developed through the persistent modest practices of ordinary manners. Just as we become robustly human through relation with others, to lose those relations is to lose something of our humanity. A familiar example can illuminate this.

The film *Cast Away* depicts a protagonist named Chuck who, after he is stranded in a plane crash, must live alone on an island for years. The challenges he faces in order to survive are several and radically distressing, but his plight is much worse because he must face these challenges alone; he is not simply left to his own devices for brute survival but psychologically marooned. But he does not remain alone long, for he turns a volleyball into a companion. With "Wilson," he converses, strategizes, and even quarrels. Together, they mark the passage of time and, in time, make their escape on a flimsy raft. When Wilson is cast overboard in stormy seas, Chuck must, if he is to survive himself, let Wilson float away, let Wilson "die," a choice he makes in utter agony, sobbing and crying out Wilson's name. The tale is terrible, but its sense and logic resides in what Wilson does for Chuck. Having a companion, another "human being"—even one imaginatively fashioned from a volleyball—is what saves Chuck's humanity, what stands between him and mere animalistic survival or, worse, suicidal despair.

What is most striking in *Cast Away*'s depiction of Chuck's relation to Wilson is how the ordinary business of interacting with a friend safeguards Chuck. Their relationship begins as Chuck is struggling to start a fire with but dried grass and sticks. "Wilson" is born when Chuck cuts his hand on a stick and hurls the volleyball in rage, leaving a patch of blood on the ball that he subsequently fashions into a face. Once this is done, Chuck has a companion in his efforts to start a fire. He uneasily watches Wilson "watching" him and, at long last, having made the fire, he explains the process to Wilson. Throughout the film, we see Chuck reasoning aloud to Wilson, as if his faculties for sorting through his challenges manifest most fully only in conversation, only with a partner who can puzzle things out with him. Less dramatically but far more tellingly, Wilson does not "sit" as a ball would, wherever he might lodge, but instead always rests, face-forward, upon a pedestal, always positioned by Chuck with care. As this makes clear, Chuck has someone besides himself to care for, to take care of, and the taking care, even when Chuck fails, sustains him. When he does fail at it—for example, once tossing Wilson away in anger—he apologizes abjectly, engaging in the exquisitely human experience of offending another, regretting it in sorrow, and seeking to make amends. In short, what Chuck has in Wilson is the humanizing stuff of relations with others, from the mundane to the profound. In watching the film, we are left to imagine that Chuck without his Wilson would have simply given up, lost the motive power and strategic sense that ultimately saves him.

Cast Away is of course a rather dramatic example of how our sociality can ground our humanity, how keeping company with others can keep our humanity intact. More typically, our sociality operates beneath conscious awareness, even as it may ground our well-being. Prosaic experiences we rarely even notice—greeting a friend, sharing a wry smile, or even hearing one's spouse humming in another room—all subtly reassure and remind us that we have others. Put plainly, much of what we can reflectively count as the good of keeping company with others is just the undramatic stuff of ordinary life. But these goods too are abundant. Indeed, the *Analects*, that text most often treated as depicting Confucius himself, frequently celebrates the inconspicuous yet profound joys of ordinary life shared with others. Its opening passage remarks the delight of having friends visit from afar.[6] It observes the joy of having parents live long[7] and of having meaningful friendships with good people.[8] It notes that even death is softened where one can die with beloved friends near.[9] These passages indicate something of the broader look and feel of the text, and of Confucian attitudes: much of what is finest and most exquisite in life is nested in the prosaic experiences we share with others. That we *need* others is no mere brute requirement, but one that renders possible what can be most rewarding and joyful in a life.

The picture of a shared life with others marked by joys and affections sustained in thoughtful interaction and companionship is, I think, inimitably appealing. I find it deeply attractive and fitting in its expression of my own personal dependencies on those I love. Yet I must also confess that were this all the Confucians offer, I would count it dreamily, fancifully optimistic. For however appealing we might find a life of robust friendship and close companionship, there is far more than this that constitutes our social interactions. In contemporary life, much of our social experience transpires with strangers who will always remain so, and our political discourse, in particular, regularly exposes us to just how unattractively fractious shared life can be. Our dependencies do not always embrace; sometimes they pinch and confine. Likewise, being in company can repel as well as attract. What is especially striking about both Confucius and Xunzi is how acutely aware of all of this they seem to be.

Both Confucius and Xunzi arrive at their high and ennobling ideas about humanity in circumstances that make our contemporary political and social climate seem paradisiacal. Their age was riven by violent political turmoil, aggression, and corruption on a scale we can only struggle to imagine. One historian, Mark Lewis, has tried to capture the depth of early China's trouble by counting the wars referenced in the classic history the *Zuozhuan*. Lewis identifies 670 wars occurring over a 259-year period and this, he is confident, undercounts.[10] The prevalence of violent conflict brought with it the great human suffering of the sort that typically attends war: poverty, violence, food shortages, and political and social instability.

Westerners may often have a mental image of the Chinese philosopher sitting atop a mountain, sagely counseling tamely attentive disciples, but life for these philosophers was far from peaceful. Confucius and Xunzi both engaged in the perilous pursuit of political lives, seeking employment as advisors to rulers who could register displeasure through violence if the spirit moved them. Their competition in seeking work as political advisors was figures such as Sunzi, author of *The Art of War* and a military counselor who legendarily demonstrated his acumen in command by slaying concubines who giggled rather than assume the military formation he instructed.[11] Neither Confucius nor Xunzi offered military advice (or killed concubines!), but their counsel was in some ways far more personally perilous since much of it involved rebuking volatile rulers for their failures in virtuous governing. Historically sound details about their lives are thin, but the modest indications tell of personal risk and suffering for their efforts. One passage in the *Analects* describes Confucius and his students hiding in the wilderness suffering near starvation, for example.[12] Both Confucius and Xunzi did manage to survive their political activities, though they each also taught students who did not. Indeed, one of Xunzi's students, Li Si, would engineer the execution of another, only to have his own fortunes later turn—Li Si's life ended when he was himself executed, severed in half at the waist.[13] In short, Confucius and Xunzi did not live on picturesque mountaintops, but down on a chaotic, dangerous, blood-stained ground.

Once we appreciate the conditions in which Confucius and Xunzi lived, their sometimes lyrically optimistic reflections on the goods of shared life with others achieve a different atmospheric quality. Their reflections indicate a somewhat wistful hope about what might be and a resolve to value what is good even when much is bad. Thus, for example, even as Confucius remarks the comfort of dying in the company of friends, he also registers his failures to have improved the world in the ways he wished. He will not "get a grand state funeral," he notes, and this is because in his own lifetime his efforts to secure a position and influence in political life ended in abject failure. In some ways, then, the optimistic hope evident in the Confucian commitment to prizing our relations with others is less about what inevitably follows where we attend closely to our sociality than it is about maintaining a therapeutic resolve. In the midst of much that is bad, it is all the more important to honor what it is good and to struggle mightily to retain one's humanity. The Confucians too, we might say, had to find a Wilson, had to devise ways to retain their humanity when much in their experience would have eroded it. I will have more to say about this later, but here it is more useful to see how despair features more formally in Confucian approaches to our sociality and manners, and for despair there are few who rival

Xunzi. Indeed, while Xunzi does extol the rewards of shared life with others, he may also be the most misanthropic optimist the world has yet produced. I confess I really admire this about him.

My description of Xunzi so far has emphasized the beauty of "nurturing" our sociality, but the greater share of Xunzi's work is in fact given over to a rather gloomy picture of human beings. Human nature, Xunzi emphatically insists, is "bad." We are "born with a fondness for profit" and "with feelings of hate and dislike."[14] Our nature is "deviant, dangerous, and not correct, unruly, chaotic, and not well ordered."[15] Xunzi's principal evidence for this dark view of our nature is that where we do not make concerted efforts to be good, we tend to be not just bad, but awful, a view surely given greater credence by the conditions in which he lived. To yield to our untutored natural impulses, he insists, produces but "cruelty and villainy," "lasciviousness and chaos," as well as "struggle and contention."[16] Whether Xunzi is correct in his low estimations of our basic inborn nature matters less to me than where he takes this dark view in how he understands good manners. Such is to say that where my own efforts to be well-mannered and attend to my own sociality are concerned, I feel like Xunzi gets me. I have no conclusions about inborn human nature, but when Xunzi vividly describes how abjectly awful people can be, I am fully on board for the ride. As much as I admire the optimistic strains in Confucian thought, Xunzi's hearty plunges into misanthropy are closer to my native inclinations.

Like Confucius, Xunzi discerns that we have great need of others, yet he also acknowledges the felt tensions our need for others produces. The plain facts of our existence dictate that we require others, but this need not and often does not entail that we will *like* them or that we will be easy in our dependencies. There is much about human beings that can be unattractive, unpleasant, and repulsive. One need only refer to one's own experience to see this: think of the last time you encountered someone who left you saying to yourself,

"What is wrong with people today?!?" For myself, that would have been just yesterday when I made the monumental error of reading an internet comment thread. My own curiosity then turned on me and I left the experience ready to hate humanity writ large. So even as I depend on others in myriad and uncountable ways, I find myself sometimes regretting this necessity. My dependencies can be begrudging, unhappy concession, something to be suffered rather than celebrated. Xunzi recognizes this phenomenon and indeed it is the founding reality for his commitment to good manners.

Xunzi often explains what good manners and civility *do* with analogies that involve bringing external pressure to bear, compelling something in one shape into another shape. For example, he tells of craftsmen who can apply careful pressure to make bent wood straight or grind a blade to make it sharp and a potter who can contour a lump of clay into a usable vessel.[17] The practices of civility and manners are meant to do this on the people who perform them: we act in ways that adjust and re-form ourselves, manners and civility operating like a potter's hand to reshape our lumpen selves into something better. These craft-based analogies invoke the need for what Xunzi characterizes as "deliberate effort."[18] The basic stuffs with which we start— be it clay, bent wood, or our ratty tendencies with others—need to be worked in order to realize their best possibilities. However, where human beings are concerned, deliberate effort is necessary not only to secure the better, but also, and more significantly, to avoid the awful. The craft analogies capture the work, but for capturing the underlying problem the work addresses, it is more useful to consult what Xunzi has to say about corpses.

Funerary ritual was a formidable element in the *li* the Confucians recommended and this explains in part why Xunzi dwells long and earnestly on what funerals do and how they ought to be organized. But Xunzi's talk of funeral rites and the treatment of corpses in particular suggests a more wide-reaching sensibility. How we interact with the dead indicates something crucially important about how we ought interact with the living. So, about corpses, Xunzi notes that

> the way that death works is that if one does not ornament the dead, then one will come to feel disgust at them, and if one feels disgust, then one will not feel sad. If one keeps them close, then one will become casual with them, and if one becomes casual with them, then one will grow tired of them. If one grows tired of them, then one will forget one's place, and if one forgets one's place, then one will not be respectful.[19]

Xunzi here makes a case for "ornamenting" corpses that stems from what they are like when we simply leave them be. In his day, as in our own, the dead were managed—washed, arranged, and rendered into a form that permitted the bereaved to take leave while protected from distressing evidence of natural decay. And, as Xunzi observes, this effort is important to our psychology.

It is of course possible to leave a corpse unaltered, but apart from the disrespect toward the dead this might indicate, such negligence will influence our emotions and psychology in worrisome ways, inspiring reactions of disgust and aversion. This will, as Xunzi notes, compromise grief, but to become accustomed to the decaying corpse is worse still. If we do not "ornament" the dead to conceal their decay, we would eventually adjust to seeing the foul result, and this adjustment is itself problematic. Extended proximity to an unadorned corpse can quiet disgust and revulsion, but in their place will come scorn and weariness. That is, our reactions will get coarser, less human and less humane. Managing the corpse, then, is managing ourselves, steering toward the sorts of reactions we want to preserve and fending off those we want to avoid. All of this of course invites the question of why we ought hang onto corpses in the first place. Xunzi clearly assumes that simply getting the dead gone and buried as quickly as possible, the better to avoid the revulsion they might inspire, is not the best option, but then why not?

Ordinarily, where we encounter something that disgusts us, the natural impulse is to flee, to avoid the source of distress and revulsion. Yet even as the decomposition and decay of a corpse can repulse, the aversion it inspires is neither simple nor unmixed. The corpse does not merely disgust but is simultaneously identified as the person we grieve. It is at once foul matter and *person*, the body a symbolic remainder of someone we care for and long to keep even as death means we cannot. There is both a push and a pull. Disgust at the natural facts of decomposition exert a push away from the corpse, while its symbolic nature exerts a pull, an attraction or, at least, a desire not to put away in haste a person still loved, even in death. Ornamenting the corpse, then, is a way to answer and honor the pull, to keep disgust at bay so that our nobler feelings of love and affection can find expression in our mourning rituals. Out of our mixed feelings, we engineer conditions to favor what is finer, our attraction and attachment rather than our disgust and revulsion. We take leave of our dead, as we must, but we fashion the leave-taking with deliberate efforts to keep intact the responses that most profit our psychology.

By now, you're surely wondering just why a book on manners has detoured into a prolonged contemplation of corpses, so let me cut to the chase: Living people are just not all that different from corpses. The living too can inspire disgust and revulsion. They too can be quite repulsive to be around. For all too frequently they do exhibit traits like those grounding Xunzi's claim that our nature is bad: People can be crassly driven to profit themselves, motivated by desires both base and selfish, aggressive toward those who impede their desires, and absolutely hateful to each other. Indeed, being around corpses can sometimes seem more desirable than being around the living: After all, at least corpses don't talk (or comment on internet threads). Because living people can indubitably be rather awful, being around them can sometimes seem to require coarsening one's psychology: sure, I can learn to put up with other people, just as I could learn to put up with corpses if I had to, but doing so can feel like habituating myself to what is most foul and unlovely. Even as I do it, I will not be better for it. But the living are not only like corpses in the revulsion they can inspire—like corpses, they also exert a pull.

Even as we recognize how awful people can be, they are not only this and they too can generate contrasting effects in our psychology. Some of their features incline us to shrink from them, but this is coupled with recognition that we find value in social cooperation, that whatever aversion living others may inspire, we cannot easily or readily forgo their company. We do *need* them and, at least some of the time and among some people, we can be affirmatively attracted. Even hardened misanthropes, after all, may yet have and prize a few friends. Thus living people exercise a mixed effect—neither wholly repulsive nor wholly attractive. This is why the disappointment and dismay they can inspire will be accompanied by a wish not to feel this way; even as they repulse us, we wish they wouldn't. Just as we long for our dead not to be foul, decaying matter, so too we long for the living not to be foul, misanthropy-inspiring louts. We do desire connection and companionship even when we find it terribly hard. This, then, forms a basis for favoring manners and civility.

Keeping company with other people can attract us and it can repulse us. Which of these effects will predominate in our responses to others, Xunzi suggests, will be influenced and shaped in accord with the conditions under which we are exposed to them. The living, like the dead, need to be "ornamented" if we are to foster fine feeling rather than low. For the living, manners and civility are the ornamentation. Rather than merely act on impulse and desire, we shape and restrain these with prosocial norms of manners and civility. This shaping, Xunzi contends, will "train and transform" desires and impulses, giving them a form and order conducive to shared communal life.[20] Xunzi's claim that manners "nurture" achieves a greater sense here. In ordering our behavior through good manners, we nurture the pull of companionship, increasing our potential for thriving sociality by behaving in ways that increase what is attractive in shared life. Displays of respect, toleration, and consideration are the ornament, effectively telling others that we are moved and motivated by more than our basest impulses.

To recast the example from Sarah Buss I raised earlier into Xunzi's idiom, saying, "Pass the salt, please" implicitly notifies others that I both prize the pull of human companionship and care to avoid reducing it in you. Rather than merely grab the salt or command you to give it to me, I ornament desire with a conventional prosocial token that marks my esteem and preference for sociality—I say *please*. Failing to do this, Xunzi might say, would introduce a whiff of the corpse to the table, subtly reducing in companions the attractions of shared company and risking increase in aversion. Saying "please" when you would like the salt is of course a modest gesture and one relatively painless to perform, but it is important to acknowledge the ambitious reach of what Xunzi offers.

If failing to say "please" carries a whiff of the corpse, it is difficult not to see much in contemporary civic life as tantamount to rotting corpses everywhere, the air of public discourse befouled by the stench of decay. Whatever "pull" toward sociality and companionship we may natively have can often feel utterly overmastered by the push of disgust, alienation, and misanthropy. This might, and surely often does, incline us to retreat from the public square—this is one of the costs of incivility. Indeed, Xunzi's understanding of the contrasting push-pull in our psychology can explain much about contemporary political life. Xunzi suggests that we need strategies to contain our disgust with our fellow human beings. And, regrettably, one of the surest ways to avoid disgust is to circumscribe our social circles, confining our interactions wherever possible to those most

like ourselves and thus easiest to like and find attractive as social partners. Whatever social impulses we feel, we will seek to fulfill them
with those we can trust not to disgust and alienate us—that is, with
those who share our values and views. Various studies following the
most recent US presidential election suggest that this is what many
in fact do: we do not reliably or regularly keep company with people
unlike ourselves.[21]

My own experience tells me that the real struggle with sociality
is not finding and prizing *my kind of people*. I have these and mostly
do not have to try to prize them or feel a "pull" toward them. The
struggle instead concerns two other, experientially distinct groups.
First, it involves simply *people*, those unspecified and unfamiliar sorts
or, most broadly, humanity writ large. My temptations upon encountering *people* are to thinking ill of humanity in much the ways Xunzi
describes. I find myself alienated upon watching a stranger cut in line
at the coffee shop or irritable at the way a traffic jam sends humanity spiraling into a Hobbesian state of nature in which all war against
all. In such cases, I know little about the people I encounter, I simply
find myself wishing not to know more and desiring to retract from
them. They are unappealing, contentious, and unpleasant in a rather
generalized way. Experiences such as these can leave one muttering,
"Ugh, *people*!" The mere word *people*, uttered in dismay, becomes a
damning commentary—to be *people* is to be an irritant, a low and
unlovely thing.

A second group, and one far more trying than *people*, is *those
people*. Unlike the largely unknown and unspecified *people* who can
undermine my sociality in rather generalized ways, *those people* have a
more definite character. If *people* provide a push into alienation, *those
people* give a forceful shove. *Those people* disagree with me, they hold
values or views I abhor, they have characteristics I cannot esteem or
even openly dislike, and they may even do things I would condemn
or organize their entire lives in ways I find appalling. I find myself

alienated when I hear *those people* avowing horrible views they perversely count as right and good or when I see *those people* going about their business utterly unbothered by the fact that they are awful human beings. Unlike *people*, who register with me as but instances of a rather free-floating unlovely humanity, *those people* are unlovely in voluntary, definite, and known ways. They register with me not as people just being people, but as people choosing to be ugly. I am, to be sure, being a bit vague in describing *those people,* but this is deliberate, for I suspect that each will have her own *those people* and mine may not be yours. Indeed, for you, I may be one of *those people* and for me, you may be one of *those people*. At issue here is the way that encountering *those people,* whoever they may be for you or me, experientially sets off *some* of humanity as a special irritant. "Ugh, *those people!*" does a different sort of mental work, establishing that there are *parts* of humanity I disdain or that provoke alienation.

The two strains in Confucian discussions of our sociality can be understood to reflect something of these distinctions where our actual experiences of people are concerned. The optimism embedded in valuing a shared life with others will often register most vividly when I think of *my people*, while the despair and alienation Xunzi so colorfully addresses will emerge when I instead think of *people* and, especially, *those people*. Yet it is also clear that our dependencies do not cleanly shake out such that only *my people* contribute to my well-being or that only *people* or *those people* can undermine it. So however appealing it might be to cosset myself by minimizing my exposure to all but my own people, life will not afford me this luxury. More deeply, the attitudes necessary to parse my sociality, to segment the social world into *my people, people,* and *those people,* are themselves damaging attitudes. Part of the Confucian project is to work against these attitudes, something I will take up in the next chapter.

Chapter 5

Living the Big Values

For the Confucians, considerable motivation for good manners and civility can be found in our sociality, from the well-being we can achieve with others to the prosaic dependencies that structure our lives. However, even as I recognize their good sense about this, there is a significant gap between acknowledging that I am a deeply social being and *living* as if it matters. It is rather easy and straightforward to intellectually acknowledge I need others. It is far more difficult to be governed by it in a robust and substantial way. For while ordinary life is pregnant with indications of our deep dependencies on others, what can or should it mean to walk around in the world with this truth? Some truths seem so deeply nested in the fundament of who and what we are that it is challenging to know how they ought operate at the surface of daily existence, how they can or should show up in how we live. Mortality seems like this sort of truth: I will die, to be sure, but what ought I *do* with that during the mundane business of a Thursday? In similar fashion, I have need of others, I depend on others, and I owe to others my very being and existence, but what does that mean while I run Monday's errands? Can I really discharge the hefty existential reality of my sociality through the conventional agreeability of good manners? The Confucian answer to this is both yes and no: yes, I really do need to be polite, but no, that's not all there is to it.

The long goal of practicing good manners is at once basic and quite elusive: becoming a good person. Perhaps the most straightforward description of what this means for the Confucians is this observation about Confucius, himself a formidably good person: After years of training and learning, Confucius could "follow the desires of [his] heart and mind and not overstep the bounds."[1] Confucius, that is, could simply do as he wished and as he was inclined because his wishes and inclinations reliably lined up with what was good and appropriate. He was not fretful, conflicted, or at odds with himself. While evocative, this description of a good person is, I find, rather intimidating and, worse, unhelpful. For a person such as myself— one whose inclinations emphatically do not reliably align with what is good—there is little guidance here. Still, the description of Confucius does offer one important tell about goodness. Being good involves working on the "heart and mind," developing one's internal emotional and cognitive stuff. I have little hope of ever becoming a *good person* in the fullest and most robust sense, but if I want to be *better*, I will need to cultivate an improved internal emotive and cognitive landscape. What that process might look like is best evident in some instruction Confucius offers to his most talented student, a young man named Yan Hui.

When Yan Hui asks Confucius about being a good person, Confucius offers that it "proceeds from oneself."[2] Asked to elaborate, Confucius bluntly instructs: "Do not look at anything that violates manners (*li*); do not listen to anything that violates manners; do not speak about anything that violates manners; do not do anything that violates manners." However elusive translating my sociality into daily life or becoming a "good person" may seem, this bit of instruction is both blunt and plain. There is no mystery regarding what I ought do—be polite and civil—yet the anticipated result is radical. Good manners, Confucius insists, are not only an expression of our fundamental sociality, they promise to transform the one who practices them. Indeed, this is the crux of the Confucian program for moral self-improvement: steady, reliable mannerly conduct will shift me internally, rendering me less prone to find to my inclinations at war with what I ought do, less given to emotional turmoil over obligations I would rather not fulfill. Above all, it will instill attitudes and dispositions that honor my sociality and what is finest in my humanity. It promises to make my relations with others more fruitful and rewarding by making *me* better in them. This importantly shifts the work of manners and civility into new territory. Practicing good manners is not simply about honoring our dependencies on others or securing the goods of flourishing with others, it is also about how my actions shape the person I am and will be.

In my own mundane experiences, every so often I find myself behaving better than I actually am. For example, I call a customer service line in great frustration, but nonetheless speak calmly and abjure venting my considerable rage upon the one who answers. Or I wish to verbally wring a colleague's neck yet maintain a professional and civil tone even as we disagree. On such occasions, my internal reality will be fractious, impatient, eager to cut loose and indifferent to the damage I might do, but my external self-presentation will evince courtesy and consideration. Unlike Confucius, I do not give my heart and mind free rein, but instead effortfully and tightly harness them. I fake what I do not feel and present myself, as best I can, as someone who is polite, as someone who is a gentler, more generous person than I am. This kind of fakery can of course seed skepticism about the sincerity of the well-mannered, but I prefer to see these episodes as minor personal triumphs, occasions in which the ratty self I am is bested by the aspirational self I would wish to be. Much of the link the Confucians draw between good manners and being a good person is evident if we consider the sorts of qualities this aspirational self includes. When I am not good, but I am *trying*, what is it I am trying *for*?

In its most general form, my efforts to behave better than I would wish involve presenting myself as *well-disposed toward others*. Being well-disposed includes, most basically, caring not to harm others and behaving as if I am steered by more than my own immediate personal concerns and aims. It likewise includes the familiar stuff in our contemporary discourse about civility and manners: showing respect, consideration, and toleration. These in turn require that I orient myself to be attentive to other people and to situations, to notice more than my own interests or feelings. I aim to appear receptive to what others have to offer, be it the mundane stuff of commercial interactions or views that oppose my own. I present myself as open-minded, receptive to navigating experiences or even disputes with others. I strive to exercise humility in my judgments and evaluations of others, foreswearing any quick leaps to dismiss, condemn, or deride that I might find tempting. I may even express solicitude for the well-being of others, wishing them well or commiserating where they encounter troubles. To behave well-disposed toward others is to appear to welcome interaction and involvement with them, to treat them with something akin to how I would treat a person I wished to befriend. In short, it is to treat them generously, as people I am *ready to like*.

As is likely clear, much of appearing well-disposed toward others amounts to behaving in accord with conventional good manners and civility. The standards and rules for these often involve just the kind of restraint I describe, a restraint that fashions conduct to appear prosocial. My appearing well-disposed is better for those who must encounter me of course, but it is also, significantly, better for me and, at least potentially, transformative.

Both Confucius and Xunzi encourage good manners because making oneself *appear* well-disposed toward others can influence one toward *being* well-disposed. Practicing manners is not simply how we *express* prosocial attitudes, it is also how we can *get* them. As philosopher David Wong has observed, the Confucians recognized early on that "there is a 'feedback loop' between the physical behavior and the emotion such that the causal arrow goes both ways."[3] Altering one's conduct to simulate attitudes one does not immediately possess can help bring those attitudes along, can prompt them into being. This gives new sense and logic to Xunzi's penchant for craft metaphors that emphasize bringing an external force to bear in reshaping an object. Just as a whetstone can grind a blade into sharpness, externally polite behavior can sharpen prosocial attitudes that may have grown dull. I may become better—genuinely, internally, dispositionally *better*—by behaving better.

Once we recognize that what we do can influence how we feel, what attitudes we find compelling to adopt, and, most broadly, what shape our internal responses to others may take, many of the worries about fakery and insincerity begin to dissolve. It can be quite beneficial for our conduct to reflect how we *would wish to feel* rather than how we do in fact feel. There is much we might say about how this process can work across the various aspects of being well-disposed toward others I mention above, but I want to concentrate on the one that most gives me fits and that seems most challenging in our contemporary social and political life: humility.

Cultivating humility is valuable for many aspects of life, but the sort of humility that concerns me involves our responses to others as these are often rooted in quick, impressionistic, and incomplete knowledge of them. A want of humility, I think, has much to do with the troubling impulse I noted at the end of the last chapter, a tendency to divide our sociality, favoring those who encourage fellow feeling and disdaining those who provoke despair or alienation, seeking out *my people* while steering clear of *those people*. Where trying to be well-disposed toward others is concerned, it will be hardest where I find myself face to face with one of *those people*. Yet I also recognize that my identifying someone *as* one of *those people* can be the product of hasty and overconfident assumptions. All too often, the ways I interpret who others are—especially where I know them little or not at all—lack hesitation, modesty, and reticence. Because of this, my sense of who they are will be inaccurate, incomplete, and, worse, wanting in charity. I see someone, form a quick impression, and draw all sorts of conclusions about what they are like, what they value, and whether or not they are *my sort*. Had I greater humility in how I assess others, I suspect, I would find far fewer of *those people* in the world, far fewer people toward whom I am quickly ill-disposed. The high population of *those people* I encounter is less a fact about the world than it is testament to my lack of caution and care in interpreting others.

Confucius notably offers several rather general comments about how we ought react where we find ourselves less than generously inclined toward others. In one passage, he remarks that when we encounter admirable people, we ought seek to be like them, but "when you see an unworthy person, survey yourself within"—that is, look to your own shortcomings and failings.[4] In another passage, he observes simply that it takes a truly virtuous person to properly distinguish good people from bad.[5] The rest of us, he implies, are likely to be inadequate judges of deep character. Confucius was also known to heartily scold one of his students who was habitually given to sizing others up with an eye toward flattering himself by spotting the flaws of others. Noting this tendency in his student, Confucius offered backhanded praise, congratulating the student on having the superior character to allow time for such pursuits while noting, "I have no time for that."[6] Whether in his general advice or his instruction to students, Confucius insists on humility in our dealings with others, cautioning against quick conclusions or, worse, eager critique of others absent thought of our own shortcomings. Most importantly, he acknowledges that our encounters with others include interpretive, evaluative aspects, a tendency to sort and order what we see of them in line with preferences and judgments we make. We like or dislike;

we esteem or disesteem; we seek out *my people* and dismiss or deride *those people.* That we do this and yet may often do it quite badly is a profound and difficult problem. To see how manners and civility can help with this, it is useful first to acknowledge the magnitude of the problem.

In discussing the temptations of incivility and rudeness, I have already noticed that, upon closer scrutiny, my impulses to bad manners generate significant self-distrust. The kinds of stories I can tell myself about my unsociable, rude conduct—that it is heroic, that it performs some high moral good in the world, that it does not really matter, or that it's all just in fun—may often be misleading. Similarly, I distrust myself when I try to reckon carefully with how easily valuing my sociality amounts to little more than cosseting myself with *my people.* In truth, I appreciate and prize "humanity" most just when the bits of humanity I engage are people who agree with me and share my values. But this should no more steer and inform my conduct than other sorts of preferences I may have. After all, that I may find sweets more delicious than vegetables ought not dictate my daily diet. Overall health—be it in diet or social relations—is not well won by systematically declining roughage. More to the point, sociality defined entirely by my *individual* preferences and judgments does not seem much like *sociality* at all, at least not a mature sociality articulated in a life that will, inevitably, include a host of others I cannot pick and choose. Apart from the undermining incoherence in seeking sociality through a heavy exercise of my individual preferences in choosing what bits of "humanity" to value, acting on these preferences will almost certainly result in dispositions damaging both to me and to those I encounter.

The most basic trouble with my inclinations to sort and order humanity in accord with my own values and views, prizing this person as one of *my people* and avoiding that person as one of *those people,* is that I am not very good at it. In my own life experience, I am regularly taken aback to discover that people defy my expectations of them. Someone I anticipate to be one of the meaner sorts turns out to be quite kind, someone I anticipate to be generous proves to be stingy, and so forth. I am not, so far as I know, an exceptionally poor reader of people. Rather, it is that my expectations of people, my sense of who they individually are, is not constructed out of a carefully formulated observational logic but from a tangle of influences I barely understand even as they do their work on the ways I socially interpret others. Social psychologists have discovered some of how this works, noting that we take cues about who people are and what they are like by reading various aspects of their self-presentation.

In his research investigating "what your stuff says about you," the psychologist Sam Gosling has identified multiple ways we "read" others through various features of self-presentation, including clothing, musical tastes, home decoration, cars, and even email signatures.[7] He conducts studies in which participants are asked to suss out what a person is like based only on seeing only the person's belongings—that is, without ever encountering the person. One upshot of this research is that it reveals how many inferences we draw and how ambitiously we interpret people by reading their stuff. And a great many of our inferences are rooted in stereotypes, associations we make about what kind of people like what kind of stuff.[8] Gosling hastens to note that some our stereotyping inferences are more reliable than others, but applied to individuals we encounter, they will ever and always be but a cognitive shortcut for figuring people out.

Gosling illustrates the limitations of our stereotyping readings by referencing the examples of Brad and Dan.[9] Based on stereotypes attached to Brad, "It was reasonable to expect he would be more aggressive than Dan." Yet Dan was the one with a "history of violence" and indeed, during the study, Dan tried to bite a researcher. Brad and Dan, it turns out, are dogs. Brad is a pit bull, a breed often taken to be among the more dangerous and aggressive, while Dan is a Labrador, a breed often taken to be among the more friendly and mild-mannered. Yet despite both genuine breed traits and stereotyping expectations attached to them, interaction with Brad and Dan as individuals is what knowing them will require. Indeed, some stereotyping impulses will actively crowd out some of what we would need to notice to understand them. Believing Brad to be aggressive, I may overlook or discount his friendly overtures; believing Dan to be friendly, I may overlook or discount indications he is about to bite me. My worry, with respect to my impressions of other people, is that I will too quickly and quite unreliably expect the worst of human Brads, that I will replace acquaintance with others with hasty, pessimistic expectations rooted in stereotypes.

Gosling's research on how stuff can signal (and mis-signal) identity intersects in my imagination with a now quaint-seeming set of remarks by Judith Martin in which she despairs of clothing bearing slogans. Of the humble T-shirt advertising a political or social view, she says that when "written statements clearly bark out orders to Save This or Nuke That, the effect is to preclude conversation in a not very polite way."[10] Martin's principal objection to such "self-inflicted graffiti" is that it short-circuits and curtails certain forms of human interaction, advertising where one stands without having been asked and reducing the chances of conversation with those who may disagree or find one's "graffiti" off-putting. Martin is worried about the sloganeering T-shirt, but Gosling's work on "stuff" suggests that we may not require such obvious markers of someone's views to be put off. Even if your shirt has no slogan, I may yet infer much about you based on it, developing quick takes about your identity rooted in stereotypes about what sort of person would wear that sort of shirt. Thus, for example, if you are wearing a T-shirt emblazoned with a country music singer's face, others may not simply take this as evidence that you enjoy the singer's music—they may additionally ascribe to you attributes stereotypically associated with country music fans: patriotism, political conservatism, low socioeconomic status. If those "reading" your identity are, say, politically liberal, they may additionally, perhaps even unconsciously, conclude that you are not their sort—that you are one of *those people*.

That we encounter others in ways that are quite interpretively active—reading others' clothing, appearance, and demeanor for clues about who they are—is a feature of our psychology and, by itself, not inherently worrisome. After all, the person who wears a country music T-shirt typically does so in part to signal something about her identity, to announce that she does indeed like that music. The trouble with our quick takes on others' identities is that they so ambitiously go beyond the evidence before us, employing a host of unexamined and unconscious stereotypes about what people are like. The country music T-shirt comes to symbolize a rich array of data points about identity that may or may not obtain, its wearer "known" in ways that far outpace what the single clue can well justify. That we hasten to such quick mental assumptions is all the more troubling given that these assumptions may in turn steer our conduct: We will interact with the T-shirt wearer as if we know far more about her than we do, as assumptions about everything from her politics to her social class inflect how we treat her. Under the power of such impressions, we may well be denied the slower interactional development of understanding that so motivates Martin—the chance to inquire, to discover, and to engage in the byplay of mutual exchange about who we are. Worst of all, we may unconsciously ground liking or disliking her based on her T-shirt. To be sure, there may exist T-shirts that would render quick dislike prudential and more epistemically responsible—a T-shirt emblazoned with a swastika, for example— but we rarely have such immediately plain tells about who other people are. Interpretive overreach is more worrisome still when we factor in how our readings of others will be influenced by identity markers that, unlike T-shirts, cannot be donned and shed at will, features such as gender, race, or age.

The stereotypes through which we read others are not confined to aspects of self-presentation that they choose, but also involve ways we are socially and culturally primed to read more fixed elements of identity. Thus, for example, when I used to accompany my elderly grandfather to his doctor's appointments, I was regularly taken aback to find that medical staff directed their questions about him to me. His visible age had them reading him as doddering and unreliable, so best to ask his granddaughter about everything from his name to his life habits, and even to how he was feeling. Or consider a friend of mine who lived in the suburbs and found that when he mowed his own lawn, neighbors he did not know would stop and inquire about hiring him to mow their lawns. For unlike the vast majority of his neighbors, he is black and was thus read as hired help rather than homeowner. In both cases, unconscious efforts to read others are misfiring by aligning visible markers of identity, age and race respectively, with stereotypes that not only do not attach, but are morally pernicious. And, not incidentally, the results are interactions that are indeed quite rude. This, then, is the great trouble with allowing our conduct to be steered by our quick takes on who people are and what they are like. Not only will we sometimes err, we will err in ways that are morally damaging.

The Confucians certainly had no access to the sorts of self-understanding contemporary psychology and social science provide. However, when I consider my own tendencies to organize my sociality, preferring those I take to be *my people* and too eager to scorn *those people*, I find use in what they offer. So too, when I worry that my interactions with others may confess reflexive biasing assumptions built on pernicious social stereotypes, I take heart that I may not be powerless to resist conduct that will inadvertently insult or affront.

Confucius encourages me to recognize that I do have tendencies, both conscious and unconscious, to size others up and that these tendencies need to be resisted by developing greater humility. I need to try to be far more modest about what I *think* I know of others and, most especially, cautious in letting disapproval and dislike develop. I could of course try to cope with all of this by engaging in laborious reflection aimed at inculcating humility in how I receive and interpret others. Yet given how much of my interpretive and evaluative activity regarding others occurs under conscious radar, it's far from clear that this would work. More pointedly, given how negatively my quick and stereotyping judgments may affect others, I need solutions that promise to bring my external conduct along toward better even if I'm not yet there internally. This, then, is where manners can aid me. Rather than allow my conduct to be steered by my epistemically sloppy and stereotyping conjectures, I accord with conventional behaviors that favor sociality and, significantly, thereby enact the humility I seek to cultivate in myself. I simultaneously treat others with greater humility and I influence my own internal dispositions toward greater humility.

The great trouble in our quick and interpretively hyperactive evaluations of others is twofold: We build robust impressions of others out of evidence too spare to sustain them and then we act on those impressions. What we need, then, is a way to slow all this down, to create hesitation in developing conclusions that will then manifest in conduct. The internal hesitation and caution we need in our judgments of others can be supported and fostered by conventional mannerly practices, by what we *do* in our encounters with others. Hesitation in internal judgment can be stimulated by behavioral hesitation. Practicing good manners does not of course entail literal hesitation, but their form is such that they can indeed produce a mental stall. Best of all, the figurative stall they provide is literally filled by conduct less likely to be harmful or injurious to others. Let me explain.

Good manners and civility are sometimes derided as unthinking conformity, as bovine capitulation to unexamined standards of social agreeability. This is in part because manners are comprised of utterly conventional and indeed often blandly regular modes for interaction. We associate good manners with unthinking conformity *because* good manners express little that is particular to the one enacting them and because they express little about the one receiving them. Indeed, this is essential to how they work. Civility and politeness, particularly with those we do not know or know well, looks much the same no matter who we are dealing with—they work like a one-size-fits-all mode of conduct. It is precisely this that gives good manners the character of a mental stall. By treating all in accord with polite conventions, I create a behavioral sameness to my interactions. Binding myself to polite conduct means that I cannot hastily enact any perception I may have that you are one of *those people*, nor can I as easily enact unconsciously stereotyping judgments of you. The bland uniformity of manners is, in other words, a mechanism for blocking behaviors that would betray epistemic hubris or pernicious biases in how I read you. I treat you not in accord with what I think of you but in accord with an external standard for treating human beings: I am *polite*. And I thus lay the groundwork for greater internal humility in my orientation toward others.

As a practical matter, where we engage others politely and civilly, we stand to find out more about them. Rather than closing off interactions, polite interaction holds them open, making it more likely that we will discover the limitations of our hasty inferences, stereotyping judgments, and unconscious conclusions about others, and be surprised by how people reveal themselves to really be. We will, in short, often discover *reasons* for greater humility. We find out there is more to that woman than her T-shirt inclined us to expect, that the elderly man can speak for himself, and that the black man mowing is our neighbor. Conversationally and behaviorally, good manners can operate a bit like a blank canvas, a space to be filled through further interaction and with detail we wait to see and discover rather than assume. And, at least in my experience, that behavioral pause often saves me from my own stupidity, from enacting judgments I will later and with considerable shame discover to have been ungenerous, unkind, or reflective of stereotyping biases I am embarrassed to possess. The important hesitation that good manners provide, it is important to emphasize, can also be helpful even where we work with information more fulsome than a T-shirt. That is, even if you present me with some pretty strong indications that you are a terrible person, good manners and the humility they encourage can be a good.

Not long ago, the comedian Sarah Silverman, who is active on the social media site Twitter, received a tweet from someone she did not know. The tweet, in its entirety, simply said: "Cunt."[11] Its sender, a man named Jeremy, managed to convey with a single word just the sort of information about himself and his attitude toward Silverman that would justify her developing instantaneous dislike of him, to say the least. After all, once a stranger has called you "cunt," is there really more you need to know in order to dislike him? Yet Silverman responded instead by seeking out more information about Jeremy, looking at the sorts of things he had said in other posts on Twitter. She discovered there that he had significant and painful problems with his back. Her response to him reflected this. She wrote: "I believe in you. I read ur timeline & I see what ur doing & your rage is thinly veiled pain. But u know that. I know this feeling. Ps My back Fucking sux too. see what happens when u choose love. I see it in you." The conversation that then ensued revealed that Jeremy not only had severe health issues, but that he lacked the health insurance to effectively address them and had been sexually abused as a child. He was, by his own account, in pain, isolated, and friendless. Silverman's responses to this additional information were compassionate, Jeremy apologized for insulting her, and their exchange turned toward a supportive effort to engage medical providers in his area to help him navigate his health issues. There is much that is fine and humane embedded in this example, but I am struck by how an uncommon impulse to civility—even in an instance when few of us could be polite—works as its starting point.

Even when people behave in ways that are patently terrible, it is at least possible that greater information about them, about their circumstances and struggles, can ground fellow feeling. Slowing down our interactions with others, creating a pause in which more robust understanding can develop, may shrink the population of *those people* by introducing complexity our quick takes too often miss or obscure. People are rarely, if ever, uncomplicated and, perhaps more to the point, people of all sorts suffer and struggle. It may not always follow that polite interaction will result in the sort of fellow feeling Silverman and Jeremy developed—sometimes greater exposure to others may well deepen alienation and aversion—but there is nonetheless great promise in assuming one's more optimistic, aspirational self, behaving politely and seeing what follows. One thereby stands to discover that people are more than one's cynical impulses, ratty conjectures, and unconscious stereotyping allow. Equally significant, greater generosity in one's interactions with others may seed greater generosity in them. This too is evident in Silverman's interaction with Jeremy, and it is one of the more significant insights in the Confucians' understanding of manners.

A full picture of how good manners can work on our becoming well-disposed toward others requires considering how manners work on others. Part of what is so striking in the example Silverman offers in her interactions with Jeremy is how swiftly Jeremy shifted in his manner toward her. Where he had initially been willing to assail her with an abhorrent sexist insult, under the power of her courteous and generous response, he changed. Rather than continue to insult her, he engaged with her and did so with an answering courtesy, rising to meet the high bar she had set. The Confucian view of good manners comprehends the significance of these sorts of shifts and encourages recognizing how trying to be a good person can effectively be infectious, influencing not just oneself, but also others, to be better.

One of the most fantastical elements in how both Confucius and Xunzi describe the good person is the sort of effects in the world they expect such a person to have. For example, Confucius says that a good ruler will bend others to the good as wind bends grass.[12] Such a ruler can act as the Pole Star, a stable navigational point that enables others to find their way. The good ruler can simply be who and what he is, and the world will be ordered and organized by the guidance his example offers.[13] A good person is "never alone" but always "has neighbors"—that is, the good person magnetically draws others to him.[14] Confucius even offers what looks like a joke about this. He fantasizes about running away from the turmoil of his society and living in the wilds. When asked how he could tolerate living among the "barbarians" beyond China's boundaries, he wryly asks how anyone could *be* a barbarian if he were there: since he is good, so will they be![15] These remarks about the formidable power goodness can exercise in influencing others initially seem to have a fairy-tale quality about them. Other people are rarely so easily bent as grass in the wind. Still, as I have already emphasized, the Confucians are no naive Pollyannas about the way the world works or even about how very impotent goodness can be. Embedded in these seemingly fanciful claims is something real and significant about how we work. Xunzi is more fulsome in describing the social mechanics involved.

All of the Confucians were deeply committed to learning and education, to arduous efforts at self-cultivation, but even as Xunzi shares this commitment, he also recognizes that much of how we are and how we behave is profoundly influenced by environment.

Whether we will or no, what we see and experience of others will shape how we develop. He evocatively describes this with reference to various natural phenomena.[16] A stubby, short plant can, despite its diminutive height, enjoy a view of vast vistas because it grows on mountaintops; a curling vine grows straight because it is set among stiff hemp plants. The important upshot of these observations is made plain when he describes the fragrant root of the *lan huai* plant: It is "sweet-smelling angelica, but if you soak it in foul water then the gentleman will not draw near it, and the common people will not wear it. This happens not because the original material is not fragrant but rather because of what it is soaked in." This is why, Xunzi insists, it is necessary to choose the company we keep carefully. Like *lan huai* root, we will assume the odor of what we are "soaked in"; we will be influenced in our conduct by what we see and experience of those around us.

Xunzi's observations about the influence of others upon our own habits, dispositions, and behavior naturally carry significant implications for what we should expect where we inhabit communities that are fractured by free expressions of hostility, meanness, and incivility. In one of his more evocative expressions, our own impulses and habits will be contoured in accord with what we "rub up against."[17] In this tactile idiom, an uncivil society is abrasive, coarse, and roughening. It will thus work to sand away fellow feeling and esteem for humanity. And this can occur without our even noticing it, the social environment we inhabit wearing away confidence in our possibilities for cooperation, shared purpose, or even coexistence. These are all risks we bear and damages we incur from negative social influences, but this dynamic also can explain the power a good person can exercise— or, more relevantly for us shabbier sorts interested in trying to be better, the power even small gestures toward better can have. Even if I cannot be fully good, I can nonetheless act aspirationally and thereby hope to summon the same from others. I have little hope to turn the barbaric good, but abandoning my own barbarism where I can may yet reduce it in others as well.

None of us have the power necessary to shift our environment in any totalizing way. We can, however, have considerable discrete effects on each other and on the ways our interactions transpire. As is demonstrated in Silverman's interaction with Jeremy, where our overtures to others exhibit generosity, respect, and consideration, we may find them more ready to answer in kind. We are, Xunzi claims, like animals in this: The virtuous person "makes his words good, and those of a like kind will respond to him. So, when one horse neighs and another responds to it, they do not act from wisdom, but rather because their natural inclination is so."[18] The likeness Xunzi asserts, from human to human as from horse to horse, anticipates what contemporary psychologists describe as "emotional contagion." Human beings are evolutionarily equipped with involuntary mirroring and mimicking processes. We do not simply see and interpret others, we are biologically inclined to "synchronize" our own bodies and expressions to "converge emotionally" with social partners.[19] As the term "contagion" implies, we "catch" emotions from others.

The process by which emotional contagion transpires is complex but involuntary, rooted in us in much way the way Xunzi suggests, as animal faculty. As the psychologists pioneering work in this area explain, there are three basic stages.[20] First, we involuntarily mimic the bodily presentation of our social partners, mirroring, for example, smiles we see on others. Second, the physical process of enacting such bodily expressions stimulates the emotions that correspond to the expressions. As the Confucians might say, the practice prompts the feeling, the external expression directs the internal reality. Finally, then, the emotion we see in another effectively "infects" us, it becomes an emotion we have "caught" from another. With this phenomenon in mind, Confucian claims about the power of a good person begin to look less like a fairy tale.

Contemporary work on emotional contagion focuses on bodily expressions of emotions and I will talk more about these in a later chapter. Here, however, I want simply to emphasize the ways interactions with others are often more malleable than we tend to think. When the Confucians ascribe to the good person almost magical qualities of influence, they are in part noticing an especially potent version of powers we all have but too rarely exercise well. In Xunzi's natural imagery, the sorts of neighs we produce, the ways our conduct "speaks" to our social partners, may summon answers in kind. Where we are polite, they are more likely to be so; where we are uncivil, they are more likely to be so. Human interaction thus has a dynamism and fluidity—indeed a sociality—all its own. When I interact with you, there is more at work than my individual character and yours. What we make of each other is not predetermined by the selves we bring to the interaction, by a fixed character we each possess, but is substantially steered by *how* we interact, the influence the nature of our interaction exercises upon us. This explains why Jeremy, in his interaction with Silverman, transitions rapidly from one who would call her "cunt" to one who would apologize and freely express his own vulnerabilities. The interaction steered him.

By dwelling on the interaction between Sarah Silverman and Jeremy, I hasten to acknowledge, I emphasize the rather extraordinary. Silverman's conduct was unusual and this is why it garnered public notice. Likewise, any user of the internet will know that Jeremy's good response is also far from inevitable. Compassion to hostile strangers on the internet does not, alas, reliably produce responses in kind. Because of this, it might seem tempting to be circumspect and judicious in our generous, polite overtures to others. Put plainly, being polite is *work*, so maybe I ought save my energies for where I have some confidence of good effects. I suspect that many of us already and unconsciously do this, paying out effort at polite sociability only where we have some expectation or reasonable hope of a polite return. Many of the reasons against taking such a measured approach are, I hope, already plain. Assuming an aspirational self well-disposed toward others can increase our ability to be so well-disposed. Rather than a finite resource we may exhaust, behaving well-disposed is a capacity that will increase as it is exercised. So too, since our judgments about who will respond well to our polite overtures may be hasty and error-prone, we ought not trust them in steering our conduct. Indeed, this is where humility is most needed. But beyond these reasons, it is important to emphasize how other people's responsiveness to my polite interaction supports the development and deepening of my own dispositions.

The American philosopher William James has a story of "faith" that I think the Confucians would have adored. If we are together aboard a train suddenly overtaken by bandits demanding our money, what happens next depends a great deal on what we think of each other.[21] The bandits are few and the passengers many, so even as the bandits threaten, the passengers could together easily defeat them. For that to happen, though, all must rise together; it will require not individual, but collective action. Yet each passenger may well not know what the others will do: if I rise, will others? James encourages us to see that there is no simple fact of the matter here, that this is not something to be settled in one's seat and ahead of any action. Instead, my standing up to resist the bandit, undertaken in *trust* that others will do likewise, can *prompt* others to do so; where each believes the others will rise, all will indeed rise. In short, to take that initial gesture requires that I have what James calls "precursive faith," a belief or trust in advance of knowing others or of knowing what they will do. This too is a dramatic example, of course, but James's reasoning reaches into far more prosaic areas of life. If I am uncertain that you like me, he suggests, behaving as if you *do* like me can work to make it so.[22] For I will be more *likable*, I will behave in ways more friendly and warm for my "faith" in your liking. The initial trust in realities unknown can summon those realities into being.

James's examples mirror the sort of dynamic Xunzi describes, but what James's version adds is an explicit commendation of faith. And it is where this faith and its good effects in the world join that we find additional support for developing and deepening an internal reality of being well-disposed toward others. To act on faith in others' good responses is to enact one's aspirational self, to elect optimistic estimations of others alongside humility about one's more pessimistic expectations of them. I behave civilly and politely—I am respectful, considerate, tolerant, and sociable—because I trust you to be. Every time it *works*, every time you fulfill my faith in your politeness and civility, I will find new support, my dispositions toward sociality with others will increase. Such is to say that every Jeremy, every horse that neighs back when I neigh, will support and strengthen my being well-disposed toward others. Their receptivity, their own answering sociality, will feed and nurture my own.

That interactions with others can bear fruit in encouraging my own internal improvement is by itself significant, but let me be a little more hard-headed about how this works on me. As I've already noted, I am not given to optimism, nor am I eager to work heroically hard to be well-mannered. I am not, in James's idiom, given to strong faith. Yet this is precisely why the dynamics that both Xunzi and James articulate work to my favor. If I can, through modest civil gestures, get other people to be more civil, I will find it far *easier* to stick with my always somewhat unsteady resolve to be better. Here too, an example is useful.

In teaching Confucianism to undergraduates, I have sometimes given them an assignment they initially really dislike. I require them to *be Confucians* when they go home on Thanksgiving break. To be a Confucian with one's family entails not simply ordinary good manners, but an especially strong awareness of one's indebtedness to family. So by requiring my students to be Confucians with their families, I am asking them to be their best selves not just as people, but as children, siblings, and grandchildren. Their responses are instructive. I have yet to find a student who enjoyed their break less for this assignment. They uniformly return attesting to having felt closer, more bonded, and in better accord with their families. Yet they likewise and significantly note that the assignment became easier as the break progressed. This is not because they *became* Confucians or so swiftly habituated themselves to polite interaction that it was fluid. Rather, it grew easier because of how uncommonly *pleasant* their families were to them: they neighed and their kin neighed back. And this, within the space of a few days, made their efforts to be courteous and considerate significantly less effort. They simply did not have to try as hard. The responses of their kin worked on them, making both mannerly conduct and its motivation easier.

The interlocking dynamics of my external conduct, my internal dispositions, and the responsive conduct of others I can inspire with my own behavior help sustain a pattern of *living* the big values I described in the last chapter. What I can externally do, what I can internally feel, and what others offer me—create systems of feedback in which, optimally, each strengthens and sustains the others. Understanding all this is part of what renders the Confucians confident that good manners, despite all the work they entail, are both possible and promising for developing ever more robust forms of sociality. What I have not yet addressed of course is the most fundamental and basic aspect of everyday politeness and civility: the specific and definite rules, the etiquette, they entail. Alas, if I am going to succeed in being more polite and civil, I cannot ignore these rules. So that is the focus of my next chapter.

Chapter 6

Rules, Rules, Rules

In his *Rules of Civility and Decent Behavior*, George Washington enumerates 110 particular rules.[1] Some of my favorites include injunctions not to kill any "vermin as fleas, lice, ticks, and company, in the sight of others" (Rule 13), and to take care when dining that you "scratch not" (Rule 90). These two rules, taken together, have me imagining some poor soul trying to eat supper while aware that a tick is feasting on his leg. I suppose that fellow, unable to kill his tick or scratch the itch, can console himself that this will aid him in fulfilling Rule 91, which reads in part, "Make no show of taking great delight in your victuals."

Washington's rules, copied from a 16th-century Jesuit manual, are interesting not least because they do forward, often in quite careful detail, what one ought to do and to avoid. Transcribed when Washington was but a teenager, both the process of writing the rules and the resulting written record of them surely operated as a kind of memory aid. For so many detailed rules entail of course that there are correspondingly many ways of messing up! Best, then, to do what one can to inscribe them into memory in whatever ways are ready to hand. Given that most of Washington's rules *are* specific, it is initially puzzling that one of the rules—significantly, Rule 1—offers this: "Every action done in company ought to be with some sign of respect, to those that are present." The broad generality of Rule 1 is curious given the specificity of many of the 109 rules that follow, and it is curious in a way that points to a wider conundrum in efforts to be more civil.

Much of what I have said so far about manners and civility concern the deep truths and profound values undergirding them, truths about our sociality and need of others, as well as the values that can sustain well-being in relations with others. These truths and values, we might say, are the Big Stuff grounding manners and civility. If I think about my efforts to be civil as efforts to translate the Big Stuff into action, Rule 1 seems a good candidate, a rule that tries to guide *by* invoking a formidable piece of the Big Stuff: respect. The conundrum arises when I pass from Rule 1 to the rest, with the ways the rest of the rules, precisely in their specificity, can seem to come apart from the Big Stuff. Some of the rules—such as exercising caution in believing "flying reports to the disparagement of any" (Rule 50)—easily track back to the Big Stuff. Yet others—such as "go not upon the toes, nor in a dancing fashion" (Rule 53)—do not clearly or obviously involve the Big Stuff at all. Regardless of how immediately sensible any particular rule may be, however, one wonders why they need each be enumerated and followed. Put plainly, if I pick up Washington's list with the aim of improving the civility of my conduct, why can't I count Rule 1 sufficient in and of itself? If I take care to "show respect," what need have I of instruction in decorously managing my fleas? This is not, for me, principally a conceptual puzzle; it is primarily a motivational challenge.

Washington's detailed instructions about the management not simply of my vermin, but of my posture in dining (Rule 96), the size of "morsels" I eat (Rule 97), the position of my lips, cheeks, and tongue (Rule 16), and the correctness of my pronunciation (Rule 73) has on me a deflationary effect. Noble aspirations to express what is finest in my humanity and to seek flourishing sociality with others seem diminished if what it means *to live them* entails fussing over how to "soak bread in the sauce" (Rule 94). So too, where I can persuade myself to motivation for seeking what is fine with others, injunctions to pay attention to how audibly I breathe (Rule 99) risk radical demotivation. The effect of all of these rules—a dreadful catalog of the arbitrary, stuffy, and tedious—is to make me lament how all the ennobling Big Stuff appears to collapse into a requirement that I become preoccupied with trifles, with micromanaging the prosaic business of eating, conversing, greeting, dress, and comportment. Such is to say that if I can get onboard for the big values of manners and civility, I may yet balk at wanting to practice and abide by *etiquette*.

Let me just recall how etiquette is conceptually distinct from manners and civility. While I introduced this distinction in chapter 1, I have largely buried it in the subsequent chapters. This neglect, I admit, owes to a certain reluctance: the longer I can talk about the Big Stuff, the more I can exist in happy denial that any credible effort to be polite must eventually end up here, talking about rules, rules, and more rules.

Where manners and civility concern respect, consideration, tolerance, and, most ambitiously, a profound appreciation of my sociality—in short, the Big Stuff—etiquette is how these broad values get translated into particular rules for conduct. Manners and civility are the *what*, while etiquette is the *how*—manners concern the larger purposes and values we seek to communicate, while etiquette maps the actual conduct and behavior conventionally fitted to them. And where the stuff of manners and civility are stable, the conduct and behaviors outlined in etiquette are changeable and exhibit great variability from place to place and era to era. They are culturally contingent, historically fluid, and contextually dependent. Judith Martin gives a useful example of the relation between manners and etiquette: the sensibilities of manners will commend to me generalities such as to "show respect in a house of worship," but etiquette, the local and particular rules in play, will dictate how this is accomplished in action—whether it entails, for example, donning or shedding a head covering.[2]

The distinction dividing manners and civility from etiquette makes good conceptual sense, but it also indirectly illuminates why, as a practical matter, etiquette can be so maddening. The noble end of flourishing sociality is attached to means that deflate high aspiration into tedium. Worse still, excelling at tedious rule-following can seem actively at odds with nobility, not least because people accomplished in the means so often fail to fulfill the end. This traces back to worries expressed by folk like Samuel Johnson and Jean-Jacques Rousseau. Adepts at following etiquette sometimes make the worst sort of human beings: both slick social operators and high-class snobs can all too easily weaponize etiquette, using adherence to formal rules as a way to manipulate or diminish people who have the misfortune of encountering them. On the other hand, clumsiness in following etiquette can bespeak a host of challenges that have little to do with lacking the Big Stuff. Some of us may, through no fault of our own, face greater challenges with the rules. We may not have learned them early in life, we may be socially awkward, or we may lack the attentional or temperamental stamina that so much of etiquette requires. And these realities of course couple with the sorts of reservations I outlined in chapters 2 and, especially, 3. The temptations to rudeness, that is, get much of their traction when we think of etiquette, of all the myriad rules being polite seems to entail. My challenge in this chapter, then, is to defend the value and importance of etiquette.

It would be nice to think that one could honor the Big Stuff undergirding civility and manners absent all the tedious and anxious rules, but, the Confucians would aver, it simply cannot be so. When manners are at their "most perfect," Xunzi claims, "the requirements of inner dispositions and proper form are both completely fulfilled"[3]— that is, the goal is to be both internally and externally oriented toward one's sociality, to be well-disposed and to evidence this in one's conduct, in the "forms" or rules one follows. The model of manners and civility the Confucians endorse reaches for nobility *by way of* the banal and ordinary; the Big Stuff is won through the little stuff. And, I am forced to concede, they are quite right in thinking so: the route to civility and manners, and to the robust values they represent, does indeed run right through etiquette. The task (not to say *chore*) is both to explain this and explain it in such a way that motivation for manners and civility is saved from the diminishing effects of instruction on managing my napkin, clothing, and cutlery properly.

I find it easiest to get a handle on the significance of etiquette if I steer away from thinking directly about etiquette and consider instead other sorts of human activity that rely on rather definite and directive rules. Scholars of Confucianism have offered some evocative and instructive analogies that help with this.

In writing about Confucian manners, Chenyang Li emphasizes the fundamentally *communicative* purposes of etiquette, the ways our behaviors speak to others, conveying respect, consideration, and so forth. In this regard, Li suggests we ought think about etiquette as close kin to grammar.[4] Linguistic competence and effective communication with others derives from structuring one's speech and writing in accord with definite rules. To see the critical importance of grammatical rules, one need only imagine the communicative disaster that would ensue if this book was "liberated" from the tedious strictures of punctuation, subject-verb agreement, and so on. Such a book might well be rip-roaring fun to write, but to others it could say little. That it makes sense to you—to the extent that it does—is a function of its following a host of rules, rules that can indeed seem dreary when one thinks of them, but that one simply cannot do without if the aim is to communicate with other people. So too, if I am well-disposed toward others and want them to *know that*, I require a kind of behavioral grammar—I require etiquette.

Just as grammar enables linguistic competence, etiquette enables behavioral competence. Making sense to others, rendering one's intentions, motivations, and purposes clear, entails, as Li suggests, appealing to ordering mechanisms that others share and therefore find intelligible. If I intend to communicate respect, I need to show it in a way you will recognize, and this is what our etiquette forms provide. Like some grammatical rules, the rules of etiquette may sometimes be arbitrary, but they are *our* arbitrary— because they exist and are commonly shared, they inform the sense we make to each other. There is no reason why waving *needs* to be a form of greeting and acknowledgment, but because it *is*, when I wave at you, you understand what my gesture says—that I see, acknowledge, and recognize you. Etiquette is the structure that allows a raised hand to do so much and this is of course an eminently practical function of etiquette rules: were we burdened to invent ways to express all that etiquette enable us to express, effective and meaningful interaction would be impossible. Behavioral improvisation might be fun, but it would leave me—my intentions, dispositions, and attitudes—opaque to others. What my gestures toward them *mean* is not mine to devise but relies on shared structures they can readily recognize and interpret. The rules of etiquette provide such structures.

A second analogy fruitfully employed to describe the way etiquette operates is dance. Robert Eno characterizes the Confucian attitude at its most ambitious as "a totally choreographed lifestyle, where the formalities of [etiquette] guided action from one's first step outdoors in the morning to the time one lay down at night."[5] I have little hope of achieving anything like the thoroughgoing grace and elegance this implies, but likening etiquette to dance does catch at additional important features of what etiquette does and how it works. Both because the rules of etiquette are shared and because we employ them in our interactions with others, they concern not simply what I do, but how what I do coordinates with what you do. Herbert Fingarette gives an example of a handshake:

> I see you on the street; I smile, walk toward you, put out my hand to shake yours. And behold—without any command, stratagem, force, special tricks or tools, without any effort on my part to make you do so, you spontaneously turn toward me, return my smile, raise your hand toward mine. We shake hands—not by my pulling your hand up and down or your pulling mine but by spontaneous and perfect cooperative action.[6]

Fingarette's description of this most ordinary yet "magical" sort of interaction emphasizes something easily overlooked, the ways we "dance" together by way of commonplace, shared conventions. My raised hand cues yours; my smile cues yours. This has about it aspects of the social contagion I described in the last chapter, but it also highlights the role of our shared rules in spreading contagion.

Much of etiquette can be understood to operate like choreography, providing us with organized steps, gestures, and movements that coordinate our conduct with that of others. It is not simply, then, about what I can communicate to you, but also about how our communicative behaviors intersect and interact under the influence of shared conventions. Like choreography, etiquette rules aim at gracious and pleasing effect but, most fundamentally of all, they ensure that one does not trod on the toes of others. Minimally, the prescribed steps, the rules, block behaviors insensitive to the reality that one shares the floor with others. More ambitiously, they enable cooperative and collaborative accord, facilitating the possibility of dancing gracefully together in common purpose.

These analogies carry distinct and somewhat different implications for how we understand the rules of etiquette. But my aim in invoking them is simply to soften up some of my hardened reluctance to accept rules. Both analogies offer familiar models of skill development in which rather firm guiding elements are essential to the products they yield, whether these be intelligible speech or graceful dance. Since being well-mannered involves communication and coordination with others, the rules of etiquette can be seen in similar fashion. Their firm guidance is necessary to ends we can count worthwhile, ends such as being understood, avoiding harm, effective collaboration, and cooperative activity in shared social spaces. At the very least, these analogies illuminate developmental needs answered by etiquette. Competent writers and graceful dancers are not born, but made, and they are made through learning processes that discipline speech and movement. So too, being well-mannered—that is, acquiring the Big Stuff—does not arrive through nature, but through learning, learning that is quite directive and disciplined. It is useful, on this score, to think again about that area baby from chapter 4 who has no friends.

The area baby has no friends because he has yet to develop the emotional competencies that come with awareness of his dependencies and sociality. The route to this awareness lies in substantial part in his being schooled in etiquette. We can of course train children by simply commanding them to consider the needs and feelings of others—that is, by explicitly telling them *what* they need to learn. This may sometimes be necessary, but it is a small part of their training. Most of what they learn is instead acquired through training in etiquette—in both explicit commands that announce blunt rules and the role modeling provided by others practicing etiquette. One need only spend a few hours in the company of small children to see that etiquette is not so bad after all. A room full of toddlers may be endearing in the free expressions of their undisciplined wills, but not always and not for long. More to the point, should toddlers remain untouched by rule or sense into adulthood, all pleasure in beholding their "freedom" would evaporate. A toddler ballet recital performed instead by adults is not cute.

When we train children in etiquette, we operate much the way Xunzi describes in his craft metaphors, shaping clay into vessel, straightening bent wood, and so forth. We bring an externally imposed "force" to bear on their native stuff and steer that stuff into a shape that is more usable and pleasing. Talk of "force" and "use" may sound rather grim and unpleasant, but it does catch at the way we initially regulate behavior from without. The goal of this external regulation is to instill internal regulation—to produce a genuinely improved shape in the child. The parent who instructs a young child to say "please," who directs a child toward seemly rather than savage table habits, or who schools a child to wait her turn forms in the child an acquaintance with the rules of etiquette. But it is a poor parent who wants *mere* conformity to conventionally polite behavior. Rather, in introducing etiquette rules, the parent imposes a behavioral structure that aims to steer the child's moral-emotional development. The parent seeks to work from the outside in, influencing external behavior precisely as a means to influence the internal: the child's attention, emotional capacities, and dispositions toward others. This is why Xunzi can so freely toggle back and forth between metaphors involving force and metaphors of "nurture." Etiquette learning really does seem to involve both. Consider, for example, the painfully frequent parental command to "say 'thank you.' "

Injunctions to express gratitude script speech—they literally tell a child what she must say—but that is far from all they do. They recommend to the child how she ought *feel* in response to the beneficence of others. The script embeds the emotion we wish the child to develop. So too, the repetition of the command does more than simply cue the relevant script, it makes connections for the child across a variety of experiences. Human beneficence comes in many different forms, so as the parent repeats the command "Say 'thank you,' " across a variety of situations, she alerts the child to patterns in experience and the emotive patterns that best answer to them. The child thus learns not simply gratitude but how to spot occasions that demand it. These features of etiquette training notably emphasize how externally imposed rules work internal good in the individual child, but such instruction is of course pitched not just at making a child good, but at making her good *with* and *among* others.

Perhaps the most significant consequence of training a child to conform to the rules of etiquette resides in the most prosaic of parental reasons for doing so: rendering her socially acceptable to others. Kelly Epley observes that encouraging a child's practice of conventional etiquette acknowledges that the "child will someday have needs for affiliation and acceptability in wider social nets than [her] relationships with [her] early childhood caregivers."[7] Etiquette will both instill feelings of sociality and enable communicating them effectively. The rules thus position the child to achieve relations beyond kin, beyond those, that is, predisposed to like and love her, making her capable as a companion, friend, student, and so forth. Put more plainly, the area baby will eventually *need* friends, and schooling in etiquette will help him fulfill this basic need of his own humanity.

Establishing that children benefit from the definite and directive rules of etiquette is, I admit, the easiest part of my task here. Far more challenging is explaining why, once I have been reasonably trained in etiquette, I need *still* to pay attention to it. After all, once I know enough of grammar or am trained in dance, what need have I to continue attending to the rules for either? For the Confucians, there are indeed some people who develop such skill that they largely outrun a need for the rules. This is why Confucius can give his "heart and mind free rein," after all. But Confucius's freedom is like that of the most masterful dancer or accomplished poet. Such exceptional people have internalized the rules to such an uncommon extent that they operate differently from the rest. Their command of sound technique is such that they rarely break with it, and when they do, it still will have an effect unlike that of the amateur. Sure, the Shakespeares of the world can largely do as they will where grammar is concerned, but few of us are like this. So too with etiquette. Giving *my* heart and mind free rein means letting the door slam in someone's face and then rebelliously refusing to apologize. I still need the rules. I may sometimes rightly need to break them, but most generally, I need them and I need to be strongly bound by them.

One of the more basic reasons we continue to need the rules of etiquette even into our maturity is that the need to communicate clearly to others abides. Sometimes, it is true, what we need to communicate to others can be frustrated by too-close adherence to etiquette, but more generally, the communicative role etiquette plays is best played by etiquette itself. Being well-disposed toward others is crucially important, but this is an orientation toward others that needs to be externalized to realize its power. The scripts and gestures of etiquette are a shared code that lets me signal my motivations, intentions, and emotions to you in a way you can understand. Thus if I do indeed *feel* grateful for a gift you offer me, and I want you to *know* that, saying "thank you" is a clear, mutually understood way to accomplish this. If I wish to drive a nail, a hammer works best; if I wish to make my well-meaning known to others, etiquette works best. This most basic point is of course deceptively basic. It assumes that I already do feel the ways I ought and I simply rely on etiquette to express myself. All too often, alas, the need of etiquette persists because we do not feel as we ought or because the early training etiquette provides starts to wane.

The pliability of human beings is what leads the Confucians to note how my sociable conduct can have a profound influence on others. But our pliability also means that sound habits must be practiced to be maintained, whether these habits are dispositional or behavioral. And, as I noted in the last chapter, the dispositional and behavioral interlock. Thus, making it my reliable practice to say "thank you" in appropriate contexts functions to keep in tune habits of both mind and behavior. It recalls me to my dependencies, enacts awareness of those dependencies, and encourages sociable responses from others. In short, abiding by the rule that would have us express gratitude where gratitude is due works to keep the Big Stuff going. As I noted in the last chapter, enacting the external behaviors that signal being well-disposed toward others can summon and encourage the internal feeling of *being* well-disposed. And what it means to enact these external behaviors will most often entail abiding by the rules of etiquette.

These thoughts about the importance of etiquette, of rule-following, involve two rather important aims: I want to be understood by others and I want to do what I can to shape my internal dispositions toward sociality. They likewise implicitly indicate ills that rule-following may help me avoid. Abiding by etiquette guards me against being *misunderstood*, against my behavior being read as disrespect, inconsideration, and so forth. It likewise protects whatever fragile dispositions toward sociality I have won against behaviors that might undermine it. That is, slack in my conduct toward others that has me enacting indifference or even enmity or hostility will work on me just as surely as behaving politely will, steering my internal dispositions in directions I do not want, not to mention tempting answering uncivil responses from others. Protecting against these unhappy possibilities is of course more in line with Xunzi's darker views of human beings. This is why Xunzi is especially adamant that we be thoroughly, utterly governed by the rules: Good manners should inform one's "meals, clothing, dwelling, and activities," as well as one's "countenance, bearing, movements, and stride."[8] This is indeed a strict choreography, but its aim is to inculcate deep habits, and no explanation of etiquette is complete without addressing the fundamental role played by habit, both the work it entails and the work it does.

All of this talk about following the rules of etiquette can be demotivating not simply because it entails concentrating on trifles, but because it sounds like so very much *work*. And it is not simply *work*, but arduous work, the kind of work that makes metaphors about forcing bent wood straight seem apt. Even so, I must concede that much of the work is already done. After all, if I wish to be civil and well-mannered, the *way* to do that is already before me. One of the keenest benefits of etiquette is that it provides a ready-made, recognizable map of behaviors to follow. Where I wish to show respect, consideration, and so forth, the work of deciding what to do has happened elsewhere and now resides in shared tradition or common custom. Etiquette encourages thoughtful sociality, but many of its customs likewise aim at a kind of automaticity where knowing *what* to do is concerned. Xunzi is perhaps the most colorful in describing how learning etiquette empowers effective action while also alleviating some of the strains of action: "One who makes use of a chariot and horses has not thereby improved his feet, but he can now go a thousand *li*. One who makes use of a boat and oars has not thereby become able to swim, but he can now cross rivers and streams. The gentleman is exceptional not by birth, but rather by being good at making use of things."[9] The *work* of the Big Stuff is here a matter of making good and sensible use of what is readily available. One appeals to long-standing custom and thereby both becomes more effective and conserves energies.

The principal work that etiquette requires, then, does not consist in deliberation but in directing myself in accord with its rules, in self-regulation. This is the real work and it is, to be sure, *hard* work, but the effort is front-loaded—again, not unlike learning grammar. One begins by learning rules of punctuation, but over time, one simply and without effort or will punctuates one's sentences. Like following grammatical rules, following etiquette can become a process one no longer registers even as it reliably structures how one communicates.

Effort is necessary in order to acquire the right sorts of habits, but the long goal is to have habit largely take over, to become so entrenched in patterns of polite conduct that they arise as if naturally, as a kind of cultivated instinct that one simply and seamlessly enacts. The power of long-standing self-regulation rendered into habit is what has Xunzi claiming, "The sage follows his desires and embraces all his dispositions, and the things dependent on these simply turn out well-ordered. What forcing oneself, what steeling oneself, what precariousness is there?"[10] Keep to the rules long enough and reliably enough, and one will no longer require conscious self-regulation or will. Long practice of etiquette renders the rules one follows second nature, displacing effort in favor of ease, and exercises of will in favor of automaticity. Notably, cognitive science seems to bear this out.

In his work drawing Confucian training into dialogue with contemporary empirical psychology, Edward Slingerland argues that Confucian approaches to etiquette implicitly acknowledge the distinction between hot cognition and cold cognition, between, that is, two distinct ways in which thought is brought to bear on stimuli and actions responsive to stimuli are generated.[11] Where hot cognition is characterized by unselfconscious automaticity, a spontaneity often emerging effortlessly from bodily sense, cold cognition is regulative, with reflective, self-conscious attention steering action in deliberate fashion. As the terminology itself suggests, hot cognition operates with quick immediacy, while cold cognition engages slower, deliberative mental processes. Thus, in Slingerland's example, hot cognition may incline me toward a second helping of tiramisu, but cold cognition will incline me to hesitate, as reflective consideration of health, weight, and so forth favor willed moderation of bodily appetite.[12]

For both Confucius and Xunzi, Slingerland argues, long practice in etiquette serves to render the stuff of cold cognition hot.[13] Etiquette practices originally feature in our experience as externally imposed rules derived from long cultural tradition and generations of practice, rules I must try to learn, enact correctly, and apply to my own experiences and in varying situations. At the front end, I need, in Xunzi's idiom, to force and steel myself, and to keep on guard in order to follow and apply the rules. I need the executive power of cold cognition. Over time and with long practice, however, the rules will no longer register as such, and what they script will instead have become akin to reflex. Thus, for example, Confucius's ease in following his heart and mind is a result of his having made hot, or automatic, responses that would originally have required cold, or deliberative, decisions about how particular experiences ought to be managed in his conduct and comportment. While aspiring to Confucius's radical mastery is beyond my ken, there is still some hope for me in all of this.

For most of us, the etiquette rules we notice are just those we have not yet rendered "hot," those rules we have not yet fully internalized as habit performed automatically. But when I canvas my own experience, I am heartened to recognize that I *do* have some reliable polite habits, habits I never notice because they are so thoroughly worked into my deep, acquired behavioral instincts. These were most apparent to me when my daughter was young, when I was regularly in the presence of a tiny person who lacked habits I had long treated as inevitable parts of my human behavior. For example, I never place my napkin on my head, but always on my lap. I do not wipe my nose on other people's clothing or even my own, but use tissue. More significantly, I do reliably wait my turn. I could go on, but suffice it to say that most of my polite habits are of this sort, relatively modest and low-lying behaviors that I no longer even notice. The hope they provide rests not in their being especially notable—I can hardly triumph in using tissue!—but in their easy automaticity, automaticity I earned through repetition. They suggest that I could make other, more significant polite behaviors routine, that I could thoroughly internalize and make hot more ambitious rules for my conduct. Exercises of will and endurance in applying rules I too often break may eventually place better behaviors among those in my repertoire of the automatic and effortless. This would, I think, yield a host of goods, but let me focus on one that I think especially important.

One of my most persistent ill-mannered vices is a tendency to interrupt when others are speaking. This bothers me, but in a distinctive way. It is of course rude to interrupt others, but what most preoccupies me about this bad habit is a worry about *when* I do it, about which people I am most likely to interrupt. I suspect that my vice is most exercised against people I unconsciously take as less important, less interesting, or less immediately agreeable to me. My vice is not distributed evenly across the population of people I encounter but instead occurs more often against people who, for one reason or another, I unconsciously or in hasty impression take to be less worthy of the deference not interrupting implies. Because of this worry, I was quite unsettled by a recent study that examined interruption in oral arguments at the US Supreme Court.

In their study, Tonja Jacobi and Dylan Schweers argue that while the US Supreme Court now has more women justices than ever, "They are given less respect than the male justices."[14] As evidence Jacobi and Schweers catalog the significant disparity in how often justices are interrupted while speaking in oral arguments. The Supreme Court's women justices are interrupted at a rate that far outpaces their male peers. Indeed, "each woman was interrupted on average three times more often than each of her male colleagues." This disparity entails not simply that the women justices are denied the deference their male colleagues receive, it also constrains the influence they can exercise in oral arguments: if you cannot finish a thought, the thought will not be heard and thereby exercise influence. To use Xunzi's idiom, women justices serially "rub up against" social conduct that affords them less respect and denies them levels of participation their male colleagues more freely enjoy. As they simply do their jobs, they are also subject to this modest but nonetheless eroding element in their interactions with peers and, I would surmise, this has an effect on how effective, confident, and content they can be in their work. At a minimum, being interrupted is unpleasant, something that makes one need to work harder simply to get one's views heard. Worse still, being interrupted can over time promote loss of confidence if one begins to think that one's views are simply not worth being heard.

If we assume, as seems prudent, that women justices are more frequently interrupted owing to unconscious biases—that is, to unthinking, reflexive bad habits rather than considered intentions— the best remedy would be for those who interrupt to develop an alternative habit. This is how I think of my own trouble with interrupting. What I need in order to address it effectively is to subject myself to the rule: *Do not interrupt others*. This will at first be effortful, requiring that I exercise executive, "cold" control over my behavior, but the long goal is simply to become a person who reliably and with no will or effort lets others have their say without interruption. Training myself not to interrupt *any* will guard against my interrupting *some* more than others, against my thoughtlessly replicating forms of disrespect that sustain inequitable treatment and leave some more than others "rubbing up against" what is unlovely in humanity. It will also work against those hasty impressions that so undermine humility in evaluations of others. Without this sort of effort, without binding myself to rule, I will almost certainly not only continue to interrupt people, I will do so unevenly and interrupt most those people who have least power or whom I have too rapidly exiled from those deserving my respect and consideration. Thoughts such as these, I must admit, render me a bit sheepish about my stubborn resistance to rules.

I am not by temperament inclined to take rules easily. Rules, after all, bind and constrain. They lack imagination and, where etiquette is concerned, enmesh me in trifles, in micromanaging ordinary experience. Yet neither can I admire my own rebellious nature where what it entails is that other people suffer its effects as damaging. However much work it is to be polite, I cannot be sanguine where my shiftlessness shifts work to others. I know what it is to be interrupted. I dislike it. I dislike the way it works on me, obliging me to work harder if I wish to have my say or, worse, to abandon my thoughts as seemingly unworthy of being heard. These are not trifles when they are *mine*, when they are the stuff of my own experience. Or, rather, as Richard Duffy observes, "Trifles are unimportant, it is true, but then life is made up of trifles."[15] The small and symbolic gestures encoded into the rules of etiquette, then, are sometimes ways of not turning trifles against each other, not making the routine, daily business of shared life toilsome and unpleasant. And the accumulation of small matters, Xunzi would remind us, is no small matter. For it bears on whether we can welcome cooperation and community with others, or will instead find misanthropy appealing, enduring people where we must but avoiding them whenever we can.

Of course the promise of etiquette rendered routine and automatic does present its own sort of puzzle. Well-mannered people, after all, salt their interactions with "please" and "thank you" and all sorts of polite gestures and scripts, and they can indeed seem to do so automatically. They are maintaining polite habits, but does it matter if these are *empty* habits, if these are not just unthinking but utterly thoughtless reflex? What we repetitively do is a puzzle in this way. On the one hand, repetitive actions influence and orient us; on the other, they can become so familiar that whatever power they once had is dulled by routine. We naturally do not mind if grammar operates as wholly reflex, but given that etiquette rules are meant, ultimately, to bind us not just to specific behaviors but to the *values* those behaviors symbolize, the dulling power of repetition seems more worrying. Here too gratitude can be a handy example.

In a chapter of the *Analects* that generally extols the uncommonly civil habits of Confucius, we are told that even when dining on simple fare, he would mindfully and reverently follow the ritual custom of making a symbolic offering of food to his ancestors, a gesture conventionally coded in early China to register one's appreciation and gratitude. This observation is pregnant with meaning. We see that Confucius experienced gratitude through following a then-common ritual to express it but, more significantly, he felt gratitude even when the food was simple and plain—when eating is most likely to be reduced to its plainest function. Moreover, when he expressed gratitude, he did it with reverence; he enacted ritual gratitude with indications that he truly did *feel* it and was not merely engaging in routine, thoughtless habit. This is, I think, the gold standard for etiquette practice for the Confucians, what Xunzi refers to as "emotion and form" aligning. What is "automatic" in Confucius includes *both* appropriate action and appropriate feeling. But reading this passage has, for me, always inspired thoughts of my brother.

When we were children, my brother was always tasked with saying a prayer before we ate. It is difficult to reproduce here what this prayer sounded like, but it was invariably the same and always said in tremendous haste. In one breath, he would say: "DearGod,thank youforthisday,thankyouforallourmanyblessings,Jesus'name,'men." If you had trouble reading that, then I may have captured the way it sounded, for except to those of us who heard it daily, it would have been incomprehensible, so run together were all the words. To be sure, for special occasions, he would insert the flourish of asking that God forgiveusalloursins—this was a signal we were about to eat Thanksgiving dinner!—but otherwise, the recitation never varied and had all the hallmarks of an obstacle to overcome quickly so that we could get on with eating. It was thoughtless, automatic, and actual felt gratitude for our food played little, if any, role. While this example concerns a child's obligatory prayer before a meal, the dynamic it captures is of course far more common. What we do frequently, we often do mindlessly, fulfilling the skeletal requirements of action but without any meat of emotion or internal feeling on the bone.

When I consider the sorts of aspirations I have in trying to be more polite, models such as Confucius are the allure. It would, I think, be enriching to feel the way Confucius appears to feel: sitting before one's sack lunch on an ordinary day yet finding in this banality the great good fortune of a world of ancestors and living others who have made my doing so possible. Living in deep consciousness of one's humanity and sociality this way is profoundly appealing. Yet were I to routinely exercise ritual gratitude before all my meals, I am likewise regrettably aware that in the mix and muddle of daily responsibilities and preoccupations, I would more likely default to my brother's model. Routine, alas, may not work alike for sages and us rattier sorts. How, then, ought I think about subjecting myself to rules that risk becoming not just habit, but empty habit?

As with all things in my efforts to be more polite, I think worries about empty habit must be subjected to some hearty self-suspicion. Because rules, whether of etiquette or grammar, can indeed be tedious, it is deeply tempting to dismiss them, to let oneself off the unpleasant hook of following them. I have seen this in students with respect to grammar, as they sometimes implore me to grade them on the (presumably) high quality of their ideas and not for trivialities such as their incomprehensible grammar. I too have sometimes felt the appeal of this artful dodge. But dodge it is. For it declines to recognize the communicative aspects of grammar, the way that good ideas will only be imparted to others if communicated in the commonly recognized forms that give them sense and purchase in understanding. There is, after all, a reader on the other end of all that bad grammar, a reader trying to interpret what the writer is saying. So too with etiquette.

Letting myself off the hook with worries of empty habit ignores the way that even empty polite habit will often be preferable to no polite habit at all where the recipients of my actions are concerned. An automatic "please" may well be—indeed, often will be—preferable to no "please" at all. Moreover, there is a great deal in etiquette for which empty habit is no problem at all: declining to interrupt others requires no special deep feeling to achieve its good effect. The rules of etiquette, put plainly, concern more than me and my feelings. The ambitious promise is that they will shape me toward sociality and greater humanity, but even when they do not, they will structure my interactions with others. So, at the very least, even the empty habit may save others from "rubbing up against" my alienating and misanthropy-inspiring conduct.

Even as I recognize the more modest salutary effect of better routine habits, I likewise think a wider issue lurks here, the issue of how *robustly* well-mannered conduct is never satisfied by mere rule-adherence. Such conduct also has stylistic features. As the difference between Confucius's offerings before meals and my brother's forced march through daily prayer illuminates, it is not just *that* one does an action, but *how* the act is done that matters. So too, at least some of the rules of etiquette themselves appear far less targeted at governing our treatment of others than at something like managing one's style—how one appears—in the presence of others. The style of mannerly conduct, then, is my focus for the next chapter.

Chapter 7

Managing the Face

After all my talk about rule-following in the last chapter, I never did return to thinking about those ticks and fleas, the vermin that George Washington implores us not to kill while in company with others. I focused instead on rules that, let's face it, are easier to track back to the big values underwriting civility and manners. It is far harder to account for rules that primarily concern bodily management, those that appear mostly to involve avoiding doing things with or to your body that may put others off. Indeed, with a careful reading of Washington's *Rules*, one can divide many of them into two distinct categories: rules that concern how I treat others and rules that concern how I manage my own self-presentation, or how I appear to others. It is into this latter category that injunctions about wiping one's mouth after drinking, not chewing with your mouth open, and, yes, not killing your fleas at table fall. It is tempting to find Washington's inclusion of these bodily regulations a bit quaint or even worrisome.

Many etiquette rules regarding the body, whether they involve using the proper fork or eating soup decorously, can seem little more than artifacts of bygone eras, reminders of a time when conventions regarding respect for others were too tightly fused with symbolic markers of social class. Etiquette manuals from earlier eras freely career between rules that make plain good sense and rules that seem only to matter if you want to look like the Quality, join the Higher

Orders, or exist in Good Company. In this way, they seem quaint. To be sure, certain forms of etiquette do still operate as class signaling, and even our contemporary civil norms regulating public and political discourse can cut toward demonstrations—or perhaps *clashes*—of class-burdened differences. This is indeed a problem, but the inegalitarian trouble with etiquette regulating the body embeds still deeper concerns; class signaling is just one aspect of a more substantial problem.

Many etiquette rules and civil norms that involve bodily self-presentation and bodily management are rooted in disgust and aversion: the rules prohibit behaviors that are likely to inspire disgust and aversion in others. This is, in part, why they can have potent elements of class embedded in them. People of Quality are decorous, refined, and alert to not behaving in ways that are perceived to be "dirty," "low," or "repulsive." Such at least seems to be a standard feature in historical instructions in etiquette, though there is of course a recursive loop in how this sort of explanation operated. Identifying a behavior *as* dirty often had much to do with just *who* was obliged, by class and economics, to do it. For example, if you share a one-room cabin with your entire family, not removing your ticks "in sight of others" may entail never removing them at all. More generally, standards of good manners that implicitly invoke disgust and aversion may involve social power dynamics in unstated ways, defining "disgust" and "aversion" in line with what people out of power do, or cannot help but do.

What societies have historically counted "dirty," "unseemly," or "disgusting" has often been turned against their populations' less powerful members. Popular attitudes that would count a behavior "rude" because of the aversion it inspires can still work this way. Breast-feeding in public remains, in some quarters, controversial, a "behavior" thought by some to repulse. So too, acceptable and unexceptional public displays of affection between lovers—such as hand holding or a kiss on leave-taking—have until recently been treated as "unseemly" if the lovers are the same gender: homophobic reactions to such behaviors often invoke disgust. These are but two examples, but the broader concern is that regulating our bodily self-presentation on a logic of avoiding what disgusts or inspires aversion cannot proceed thoughtlessly and insensate to how culturally conditioned disgust can be, to how our disgust reactions can embed noxious prejudices and inequities. Even as I count this worry profound, I nonetheless think that bodily management must play a role in what it means to be civil and polite. Put more precisely, bodily management *already* plays a role in how our social interactions transpire, so we best try to get smart about how it works and see if we can't bend it toward the good.

Both Confucius and Xunzi clearly assumed that management of one's self-presentation, of one's body and its expressions, was an ineluctable element of being well-mannered. Xunzi, to recall, claims that good manners ought infuse one's "countenance, bearing, movements, and stride,"[1] and the *Analects'* presentation of Confucius's own mannerly habits often make reference to his body, noting his posture, the direction of his gaze, and manner of sitting, for example.[2] Some of the attention paid to the body by the Confucians clearly involves the Big Stuff, the deep values underwriting ordinary polite and civil behavior. Thus, for example, that Confucius does appear solemn in making his offerings before meals is testament to his internal workings, it is evidence that he possesses deep dispositions regarding human dependency and sociality. I think the Confucians expected that if you genuinely *feel* the Big Stuff, it will tend to show up in your bodily expressions. But there is more to it than just this, for even before we have our dispositions in hand, we will need bodily regulation, and this does indeed owe to worries about inspiring aversion in others.

The Confucians were no better than most of history's etiquette advocates in clearly separating social power dynamics from how they conceived what might disgust or inspire aversion. Nonetheless, I find much in Xunzi that enables me to think about these issues in what I hope is a more egalitarian way. When I consider our capacity to inspire aversion in others, my thoughts trace back to Xunzi's remarks about how we should manage corpses and to the likeness I see between corpses and living human beings. The aversion I worry about attaches to our sociality, to the ways that the bodily expressions of others can undermine appreciation of our deep dependencies, reducing our confidence in the value of shared life with others, willingness to cooperate with others, and, most basically, our interest in being in company with other people. The worry, in short, is that our bodies can make us corpse-like to others, a source of dismay and revulsion that will have us wanting to flee from other human beings into solitude.

To recall, Xunzi claims that a corpse should be "ornamented" in order to allow the bereaved to mourn, to take leave of the dead without undue haste while protected from sight of the corpse's decay. It is good for us—psychologically, morally, and emotionally—to honor our attachments to our dead, but to enact that good requires engineering conditions to guard against physical realities that would put us off it. In all this talk of corpses resides a dynamic also evident in our relations with living others. Unornamented by the restraining power of manners, they too can put us off, inspiring misanthropy and alienation. And this too is bad for us: insofar as others inspire aversion, they will erode our interest in cooperation, in community, and in shared life with others. So far, this but recapitulates what I offered in chapter 4, but here I want to dwell on how potently bodily management and bodily expression influences whether we will find the company of others appealing. I don't think we have to look hard to find examples of how this operates, but let me lead with one from the *Analects*.

In *Analects* 2.8, one of Confucius's students has asked him about filiality, about the particular forms of respect given elders and, especially, one's parents. Confucius replies, "It is the expression on the face that is difficult. That the young should shoulder the hardest chores or that the eldest are served food and wine first at meals—whenever was this what filiality meant?" Confucius is suggesting that to be filial, one cannot merely abide by the established conventions for doing so, one must also manage one's face. To translate this into a more contemporary idiom: parents of teenagers everywhere, Confucius knows what you are going through. A child who takes out the trash as instructed, but does so with that face known to all parents—the *fuck you* face—is not really succeeding if the aim is to perform well-motivated help around the house, much less to demonstrate consideration in sharing the work of the household.[3] The trash is removed, but the face can put one off, can undermine or nullify the cooperative aspects of the deed. Indeed, it can make one prefer to carry the trash out oneself just to avoid the company of a surly teenager begrudgingly, resentfully obliged to do it.

As Confucius's remarks about the face suggest, the body sends communicative signals and sometimes *what the body says* can undermine the value and meaning of an action. Because of this, regulating the body is quite often *part of* being polite, part of whether our effects on others cut toward encouraging robust sociality or inspiring alienation. Indeed, in some cases, inapt bodily expression can utterly cancel an action that would, in any superficial outline, be polite or civil. Thus, for example, it is polite to apologize when one has wronged another, to condole with the bereaved, and to avoid interrupting when others are speaking. These are sound, generally reliable rules, but we in fact need more than the plain rules describe to fulfill what they indicate. Indeed, we might say there is a hidden rule residing underneath many of our most significant etiquette rules: look like you mean it. That is, you need not only to perform polite behavior, you need to *perform* it, making your conduct stylistically hit the expressive register conventionally associated with the rule you follow. Above all, you need to avoid adopting any bodily style that fouls the act: do not apologize through gritted teeth while sneering; do not condole with the bereaved while smiling and laughing; do not forgo interrupting only to sigh audibly and roll your eyes while another speaks. Significantly, these stylistic failings may well reverse the action one ostensibly performs. If I apologize through gritted teeth while sneering, have I, in fact, *apologized*? Can the style of my apology turn the act of saying, "I'm sorry" into its reverse, into a refusal to apologize? One's bodily style, in short, matters— indeed, it can matter so much that it defines what act one has in fact performed.

Apologizing, condoling, and not interrupting are cases in which inapt bodily expression can work to undermine, negate, or reverse the "good manners" of an action. About genuinely good manners, there are *both* rules to follow and *ways* they must be followed. In these sorts of examples, the principal trouble is how one's bodily style inflects what one communicates to the person receiving the gesture. If my aim truly is to condole with the bereaved, I will *want them to know that*, I will want to deliver my sympathies in a manner that effectively conveys what I intend. To be sure, sometimes we intentionally set the letter of law against its spirit, deliberately styling a formally "polite" gesture to show that we don't in fact really mean it. Sometimes we apologize through gritted teeth precisely to demonstrate our lack of regret or indifference to trouble we've caused others. But such moments of nefarious ironic "politeness" perversely reinforce the underlying significance of bodily style. They show how potent it is in defining what we will communicate. Thus, whether my aim is to sincerely apologize or to sardonically insult via "apology," the recipient will garner much of what she understands about my intentions from how I "manage my face," by the way I do what I do.

How I style my conduct will influence how you interpret my various gestures toward you, but the challenge and trouble of style does not end here. All of my examples so far involve direct person-to-person interaction, but alas, the communicating force of our bodily expressions is felt by more than just those at whom we directly aim it. Our bodies are so persistently sending signals to others that we are effectively communicating even when we are not obviously interacting with others at all. Xunzi's claims about the effects of what we "rub up against" are relevant here. In social spaces—that is, anywhere we are in the presence of others—how we comport ourselves physically can subtly inflect and influence what others experience. And Xunzi would argue, this can in turn inflect and influence how well-disposed others will be toward us and, more importantly, humanity writ large. This is best captured with another example, one that illuminates how even when we are not directly interacting with others, we may yet introduce a whiff of the corpse into a social atmosphere.

Consider a busy coffee shop in which the customers are abiding by customary etiquette, forming a line for service and each waiting her proper turn to be served.[4] By itself, this is a kind of triumph of "ornamentation." After all, a coffee shop is a place where people with animal needs assemble: each will want what she wants, each would prefer her wants to take priority over others', and each would enjoy immediate gratification more than suffering delay. Yet despite all of this, they collectively form a line. The formation of a line is, Xunzi would offer, a way to pattern into order the raw desires in play, a strategy for controlling the way in which each person seeking coffee is exposed to the desires and interests of her fellows. Minimally, the formation of a line reduces the potential for competition and exercises of brutish power. Maximally, however, it seeks to bar the aversion to others that unchecked, unrestrained display of our base needs and interests can generate.

Human beings voluntarily forming a line and awaiting their turn to be served is, in Xunzi's idiom, an adornment of the desires that draw people to the coffee shop. They do not merely decline to compete, but also implicitly encourage each to see each as more than animal stuff governed by brute processes. Those present have cut short the raw, animal desire for coffee and extended the desire for cooperative sociality, giving greater play and expression to what will render them more agreeable to others.[5] That we form lines rather than try to stampede over each other in brutish efforts to be first can subtly incline us to think better of humanity, or at least minimize any tempting misanthropic impulse. But all of this so far involves the mere fact that we wait our turn. In truth, the sorts of good effects that can be won by a group of strangers waiting their turn can be undermined or even overturned by stylistic elements, by atmospheric crosscurrents created by body language.

Just as someone who breaks in line can rupture the fragile prosocial atmosphere of a coffee shop line, so too can one's *manner* of waiting one's turn. For example, stuck in line behind an elderly patron who pays for his coffee by laboriously and slowly writing a check, I may huff with impatience and roll my eyes, shift my weight from foot to foot and conspicuously check my watch. I may observe a harried parent burdened by restive small children, and mutter to myself in irritation while casting irritable, judgmental glances at her progeny. Finally, impatient with waiting, I may decide to while away my time awaiting coffee by opining loudly into my cell phone, treating all present to my thoughts about the news of the day as I relay them at high volume to the person on the other end of my call. While such behaviors do not overtly violate explicit rules of etiquette, they nonetheless violate mannerly sensibilities. They do indeed introduce that whiff of the unlovely corpse. Just as a literally unpleasant smell would do, they can shift the experience of waiting for one's coffee, rendering it an occasion of exposure to what is more raw and less appealing in human beings. Let me dwell on this just a little, if only to unearth the effects this sort of thing has on me and thereby amplify my incentives to avoid being the corpse among the living.

Most basically, a demeanor that communicates impatience with the elderly, intolerance of the young, and indifference to the presence of others represents an incompleteness or incomplete success in ornamenting raw desires. Demeanor can indirectly confess: I want my coffee *now* and others are mere obstacles to my wish, *unpleasant* obstacles standing between me and my comfort and convenience. I abstain from violating formal etiquette—I do not break in line—but my demeanor and manner announce the heavy cost of my restraint, how very little I care for others' needs and interests as these interfere with my own, and how much, put plainly, I wish all others would simply *get out of my way*. How I wait for my coffee thus transmits micromessages, texturing others' experience of "rubbing up against" my desires. Where those micromessages convey reluctant, resentful, and hostile acceptance of restraint on my desires, I may succeed in remaining tolerable, but I will not be *appealing*. My demeanor can tempt misanthropy, subjecting others to what is baser and displeasing in being among others. The worry here is that cooperative and collaborative sociality will be undermined where being with others registers as unpleasantness, even mild unpleasantness, to be endured.

By now, I expect, I have utterly lost some readers, readers who will find all this fretting over physical demeanor in coffee shop lines just too much. It is bad enough that I suggest we do indeed need to abide by etiquette rules, and now I am condemning a little harmless expression of impatience in coffee shops. To these readers, let me say that I get you, that I share your dismay and that I can huff in impatience and roll my eyes with the best of you. Yet I also must allow that Xunzi's attention to the aesthetic, stylized features of our conduct plays upon me and disturbs me. And it does so precisely because I have misanthropic tendencies. These tendencies entail that, put plainly, it does not *take much* to put me off wanting to be in the company of other human beings. Even as I despair of regulating my own demeanor, I surely would like others to do better at regulating theirs. For this would go a great distance in checking my always-eager impulses to dislike them, to dislike humanity writ large. And this, I think, is the crux of Xunzi's concern.

Xunzi appears ready to see the awfulness of human beings, ready to see the pains and despair inspired by being among them. He discerns that a coffee shop in which demeanor is "ornamented" with prosocial signaling will subtly protect those present from the disdain, scorn, and distaste human company can induce. The less we must "rub up against" the brute, the chaotic, and the self-focused, the less tempting misanthropy will be. More ambitiously, were we able to better ornament our conduct, we would have a chance at communities in which we find the company of others not merely tolerable but pleasing. That is, Xunzi recognizes the significant difference between being able to *endure* other people and finding human company *appealing*, between begrudging acceptance of our dependencies and deriving meaning and sustenance from them. However much I quail at managing the thorough self-regulation he endorses, I likewise cannot help but see how powerfully influenced I am by exactly the sorts of experiences that concern him. Here too, contemporary research seems to bear out Xunzi's interest in the style of our social conduct.

Scholars who study workplace conditions have observed multiple ways that relatively subtle bodily cues can influence both group dynamics and individual performance. Bodily expression is a formidable force in social contagion, in our assuming the emotions and moods of those with whom we interact. For example, Sigal Barsade has studied how both positive and negative emotions may be "caught" in working groups. Using an actor trained to exhibit a variety of nonverbal cues while hewing to a consistent verbal script within a group activity, Barsade found that "people are 'walking mood inductors,' continuously influencing the moods and then the judgments and behaviors of others."[6] In Barsade's study, "hostile irritability," "depressed sluggishness," "cheerful enthusiasm," and "serene warmth" —all delivered via nonverbal signals—steered the study participants toward mirroring moods.[7] Working with someone exhibiting hostile and irritable body language will make you more prone to hostile irritability. Put simply, empirical research bears out what many of us already discern in our experiences: rubbing up against the emotive and attitudinal texture of others' conduct influences us, for both good and ill. How they stylistically inflect their conduct matters to what we make of our experiences with them and how we feel in those experiences.

Once we realize that the style of our conduct can indeed inflect our interactions with others and that it can influence the felt atmospherics of shared social spaces, we have considerable incentive, I think, to aim for greater bodily self-regulation or, in Confucius's idiom, to manage our faces. The goods such efforts accomplish are multiple. Most basically, where I can use my body's expressive capacities to communicate prosocial attitudes to others, I hook into just the sorts of dynamics the Confucians are eager to promote. Adopting prosocial bodily expressions even where I don't feel especially prosocial can bring those feelings and dispositions along: the external can influence the internal. Likewise, because my moods and emotions can be "contagious," my prosocial demeanor can influence others to answering prosocial demeanors. Not only will I not inflict my bad moods on others, but their answering in kind where I signal being well-disposed provides just the sort of feedback that will strengthen my efforts to *be* more genuinely well-disposed. These effects primarily concern how I will be improved by regulating my body, but what most motivates me is the prospect of doing less damage in the world than I otherwise would.

Some days, I confess, I feel like a Typhoid Mary, my inability to manage my face where my attitudes are at their worst infecting all I encounter with my surly antisocial mood and poisonously hostile emotions. By itself, this would be bad enough, but I am also acutely aware that our bodies' expressive capacities can work against some of our most noble moral aspirations. Where we want, for example, to live in a world organized by principles of human equality and dignity, the body can betray us. This owes to multiple factors, including our hasty judgments of others, unconscious pernicious stereotyping, and poor habituation. The body's betrayal of our better intentions and consciously endorsed values is one source of damage we can unthinkingly deal others. Where all of us will sometimes be Typhoid Marys, not all of us will be subjected to the same types or levels of infection. Some of us are exposed to more toxins than others; some of us are obliged to "rub up against" coarser and rougher social behaviors that undermine confidence in shared humanity. Let me give a couple of examples.

When I worked as a housekeeper, I was sometimes paired by my agency with other housekeepers. Some jobs just take two, and so I would work jobs with other housekeepers, invariably, given my youth at the time, ones older and with greater experience than I. Despite my lesser experience and comparable youth, it was commonplace for our clients to direct themselves to me, whether this involved their offering pleasantries and casual conversation or in order to issue directives about what services they wanted performed. They would make eye contact with me but not my partners, they would tell me rather than us where we might leave our belongings while working, and so forth. Even if my partner asked a question, chances were the client would direct the answer to me. When clients did speak to my partners, their speech would typically be louder, more summarily commanding, and noticeably more condescending, absent the softening gestures and tones they used with me. At worst, clients would more frequently "stalk" my partners. Some clients do not trust housekeepers not to break or steal things or to be slipshod in their work, and I expect every housekeeper has been stalked through a house more than once, the watchful, suspicious homeowner eager to protect her goods from the woman paid to clean them. But when I worked with partners, it was invariably they and not me who would be stalked by clients inclined toward stalking.

Initially, these patterns of my working life made no sense to me. Eventually, far too belatedly, I recognized the fundamental difference between myself and my partners: I am white and they were Latina. The myriad differences in body language and style of address were but the product of racialized stereotypes showing up in a host "trifling" ways. I got the pleasantries, the softening verbal and nonverbal gestures, and small talk because our mostly white clientele identified with me—I awakened whatever internal magic cued more prosocial behaviors. My partners, in contrast, summoned up in them the dark magic of unacknowledged and likely unconscious racial biases that in turn manifested in bodily expressions and style that communicated those biases. Few of these clients, I believe, harbored consciously endorsed racial biases—that is, they would likely disavow explicit racial bias—but their manner of interaction distinguished my partners from me. With me, they were at greater ease, more friendly, and less suspicious; with my partners, they were patronizing and imperious in tone, wary and watchful in behavior. Subtle differences of this sort are perhaps most powerfully caught in accounts given by black men.

George Yancy has coined the expression "elevator effect" to describe what it is like to be a black man sharing an elevator car with a white woman.[8] The effect is derived not from explicit communication, nor is it deliberately inflicted. Rather, it transpires through a woman's bodily tension, her visibly gripping her bag more tightly, her failure to make eye contact, and so forth. Even though nothing is said, Yancy argues, "Her body language functions as an insult."[9] A similar pattern is evident in an account offered by the journalist Brent Staples. When Staples was a student, walking in his university neighborhood schooled him in unanticipated ways: "I became an expert in the language of fear. Couples locked arms or reached for each other's hand when they saw me. People who were carrying on conversations went mute and stared straight ahead, as though avoiding my eyes would save them."[10] Staples painfully describes the multiple strategies he pursued to avoid inspiring fear in others. Smiling had no effect, he "tried to be innocuous but didn't know how," and he would detour "into side streets to spare them the sense that they were being stalked." Eventually, he landed on a strategy that worked: he would whistle Vivaldi and would watch as the "tension drained from people's bodies when they heard me. A few even smiled as they passed me in the dark." When Staples whistled Vivaldi, others would take this bit of cultural sophistication as a signal that although he was black, he was also a university student and thus not to be feared.

In both Yancy's and Staples' accounts, stereotyping of the black man as potentially violent and a source of fear are appearing in a host of nonverbal signals. The bodies of those they encounter are registering perception of threat and, most significantly, they thereby *communicate* fear to Yancy and Staples. These bodies speak and what they say embeds long-standing pernicious stereotypes regarding black men. Moreover, as Yancy argues, the issue here is not simply the message of the moment, an experience he describes as "confiscating" his identity by rendering him into racialized stereotype, but that such encounters are serial—they happen repeatedly and persistently, creating cumulative effects that stretch out over a lifetime of days and years.

In Xunzi's idiom, both my housekeeping partners and Yancy and Steele are obliged in their ordinary life activities to "rub up against" the coarse realities of pernicious racial stereotypes and biases. Confidence in shared humanity, meaningful community, and social cooperation are sanded away with every encounter. The profound worry here is that such experiences leave those who suffer them alienated, altering for the worse what perspectives about humanity they can readily find plausible and possible. Subject to such abrading encounters, one cannot celebrate or rejoice in human dependencies or develop ever more robust sociality; one wants instead to find the "side streets," ways to simply steer clear of what is most unpleasant and unlovely. In these cases, the expressive power of the body is working to inspire a righteous aversion to human company, a disgust that has strong moral and existential features. Welcoming interaction with others requires that one not frequently find one's own humanity discounted, overlooked, or, in Yancy's idiom, "confiscated" into longstanding pernicious and dehumanizing stereotypes. Let me pull away from these examples and explain just what work they do on me in my efforts to be more polite.

Where issues of pernicious stereotyping biases are concerned, "be polite" seems decidedly weak tea, a remedy too modest for the malady. Yet as these anecdotes attest, inattention to bodily expression leaves intact and unamended modes of interaction that are morally and socially deeply undesirable. The physical self-discipline that good manners entail will likely never be adequate to address the trouble here, but it may reduce it. For while managing the face and regulating bodily expression may not directly repair underlying, unconscious biases, it would at least contain the toxins, sparing others exposure to what will infect their experience in ways that undermine sociality. The long goal, the Confucians would have us expect, is that attitudes, dispositions, and emotions too would begin to shift as bodily practice does its work on our internal mechanics. Above all, a commitment to manners and civility does substantial work simply by *putting in view* the significance of all our many "trifles." By this I simply mean that one of the more substantial barriers to changing social atmospheres is neglect of the myriad ostensibly modest currents and crosscurrents they include, the ways atmosphere can shift on the slightest breeze. What attention to the body's expressive capacities can do in this regard is begin to direct some of the currents.

Of course the inevitable doubt that lingers for me in considering my own bodily management is just whether or how much I truly have control over my physical expressions and thus what they communicate to others. Xunzi is adamant that we do indeed have considerable control, control that is most evident in those who have fully mastered themselves. He claims that for a virtuous person, moral learning "enters through his ears, fastens to his heart, spreads through his four limbs, and manifests itself in his actions. His slightest word, his most subtle movement, all can serve as a model for others."[11] I expect he's right that the "softest words" and "slightest movements" can be dense with meaning, but since I am not virtuous in the robust sense he describes, I do not find my good intentions yielding the totalizing harmony Xunzi describes. Rather, I can mean well and yet manage still to mess up in considerable ways. The body speaks, to be sure, but it also betrays. It can fail to live up to the aspirational aims I have in myriad ways. I can feel remorse yet apologize badly; I can forgo interruption yet find myself sneaking a peak at my watch; I can be setting off to think about good manners and let a door slam in someone's face; and, I am uncomfortably aware, I surely do physically comport myself differently with different people, unsure even of what those differences are and what they're inflicting on the others I encounter. Put plainly, of all the work improving my manners entails, here is where I am least confident that I can take myself in hand and do significantly better.

Perversely, I think my lack of confidence that I can well manage all that must be managed to make my body work to the favor of better manners is itself an asset of sorts. One of the greater troubles in managing our bodies well, I expect, is thinking we are fine just as we are—that is, in failing to see the work before us. In this way, we can be akin to exceptionally bad dancers leaping and cavorting wildly under a mental trick that has us believing we are master ballerinas. Lacking confidence may attest at least to my having got past this bit of self-deception. Attending to all that robustly good manners entail requires recognizing one's failings and weaknesses, all the ways we oblige others to rub up against our crashing, clumsy ineptitude.

So too, I find some consolation and indeed optimism about my capacities to regulate myself by returning to George Washington's many rules. Much of what he offers regarding the body is, to be sure, the stuff I find hardest to credit as mattering most. But I am struck by how much of what he instructs, I have already mastered. I do not "in company, put [my] hands to any part of the body not usually discovered" (Rule 2). I do not speak while yawning (Rule 5); sleep when others are speaking (Rule 6); stare at "the marks or blemishes of others" (Rule 71); or talk with my mouth full (Rule 98). Such is to say that much of what we count most basic in table manners and well-mannered bodily management is stuff I have well in hand. And these patterns of bodily management were never inevitable, but learned and then internalized. They thus testify to my own potential, suggesting that I *can* indeed develop better bodily habits, that there is promise in trying. As with subjecting myself to the rules of etiquette, I must work to develop prosocial bodily practices. But, as with etiquette, the work will be supported by the answering effects I may solicit from others and, more basically, by the hope that in doing the work, I will be contributing to world in which misanthropy is less compelling.

In articulating my own orientation toward bodily practice, I should note, I have largely steered away from the more primitive forms of disgust and aversion encoded in traditional etiquette and civility writing. My own concerns about bodily management center on *symbolic* micromessaging—bodily expressions that convey disrespect or inconsideration of others, or that set some apart—rather than on any more raw or base "ick factor" some bodily expressions may awaken. In truth, I retain reservations about the presumptively more primitive forms of disgust and aversion. On the one hand, I can certainly see the prudence of schooling children not to wipe their noses on their clothing and of not chewing with my mouth open, but, on the other, my historical sensibilities cannot let go the suspicion that too much of what we count "proper" in bodily management is burdened by socioeconomic class hierarchies and by worrisome cultural biases of various sorts. This suspicion preys upon me in ways that preclude treating bodily management in traditional fashion, where disgust and aversion are assumed to register reactions to bodily aesthetics taken as general. I doubt that we do have many truly primitive and thus generalizable "ick" reactions, reactions somehow native to human preferences rather than culturally conditioned. More importantly, I doubt that the long goals of good manners are well served by indulging in policing behaviors that may appear to inspire such reactions. Let me explain.

When we consider the ways in which failures in bodily management can inspire aversion or disgust in others, I think it crucially important to register the sociocultural conditions in which such reactions can take hold. For example, much of what I say about the physical symbolics of how we wait in line for coffee would surely need to be modified if I were instead addressing how people in conditions of deep deprivation wait in a bread line for resources that are scarce and without which their base well-being will be threatened. A world of waiting in line for coffee is, in short, already a pretty good world. In contrast, maintaining a prosocial aspect in one's countenance where structural and material realities do not favor base survival, much less thriving community, is a different sort of task. One will yet *need* community—indeed the need for community is amplified—but the trouble here is predominantly macro, having to do with a world in which deprivation can set some in conditions where material needs are not readily met. The micromessaging of good manners is the least of our troubles and so should not summon more of our attention than the wider realities in which people may be situated. In short, I am impatient with accounts of manners that would scold or deride the "poorly behaved" where these are people in conditions of deprivation their critics have never faced. This impatience, I think, must be *part of* being well-mannered in any robust way.

Undergirding my treatment of good manners in this book is a dedication to working on myself, a Confucian-inspired devotion to *self*-cultivation. Part of this dedication includes, as I have already outlined, a commitment to humility where my evaluations of others are concerned. This humility, I find, is crucial to matters of the body. Economic conditions inform how our bodies operate in the world, constraining not simply where we may need to remove our ticks, but what sorts of social self-presentation are available to us. So too, bodily health, age, class, race, and even physical size condition how we will appear to others. My own sense is that the greater peril in matters of the body is that we mistake managing our bodily expressions for license to police the bodily expressions of others. What I want in my own good manners, then, is twofold: I want to manage my bodily expressions against disregard of other people and I want not to be hasty and ungenerous in how I read the bodily expressions of others. I want, in short, my work on the body to be about *my* body, not yours.

Ungenerous judgments of the bodies and bodily management of other people already, I think, enjoy too much purchase in our ordinary lives. We may freely mock the Victorians for their obsessions with table manners and bodily propriety, but our own cultural environment can encourage distaste with the bodies of others based on aesthetic sensibilities honed by a mass popular culture that floods experience with images of people refined away from what we typically encounter in the world. We are, moreover, encouraged to forms of body policing that answer to no higher purpose than a dubious conformity to a standardized and altogether too narrow range of aesthetic possibilities. Perhaps because I have achieved a certain age, I increasingly notice articles and internet posts purporting to school me on what women my age should never wear, hairstyles thought unsuitable to my years, and a thousand different strategies for appearing less like what I in fact am, a middle-aged woman. The effects of such cultural messaging are of course well investigated by scholars in a variety of academic disciplines. My concern with them, and with their myriad variations pitched at all sorts of people beyond middle-aged women, is how they calibrate our sense of bodily management and, most especially, our willingness to cast an ungenerous, ill-mannered eye upon the bodies of others. They ill suit us for encountering the rich variety of human bodily possibility and risk rendering us rude in how our own bodies micromessage disapproval of others' bodies.

The sorts of bodily practice and bodily experience that most disturb me are well captured by the photographer Hailey Morris-Cafiero. A few years ago, Morris-Cafiero posted online a series of photographic self-portraits, pictures of herself out in the world in a variety of contexts, and the origins story of these is instructive. Morris-Cafiero, who is overweight, began the project when she took a series of self-portraits only to discover upon developing the film that in one "there was a man behind me and he appeared to be sneering at me."[12] She continues, "And then it happened 5 minutes later on the same roll of film." Thus began Morris-Cafiero's "Wait Watchers" project, a robust series of self-portraits, each of which features Morris-Cafiero simply out in the world engaged in ordinary activities but also, owing to her weight and self-presentation, subject to body language in others that conveys disapproval, disgust, condemnation, or aversion. One, for example, features Morris-Cafiero simply eating gelato while a young woman looks on with a furrowed expression.

In another, Morris-Cafiero sits on some public stairs while a young man behind her poses for a picture clearly meant to include her in it—his lips pursed smiling, his eyes downcast at Morris-Cafiero, his face registering a mocking consideration of her body. This, in a nutshell, is what most troubles me about how easily some forms of aesthetic interest in the body can trip into just the forms of rudeness I have dwelled on in this chapter. Both portraits palpably suggest that there is something wrong, ill-ordered, and aversion-inspiring in a woman on the street eating a gelato or resting on a staircase, a wrongness that is only possible to locate with reference to the type of body Morris-Cafiero has.

The forms of disgust and aversion Morris-Cafiero's work evocatively suggests do appear to be raw, baser forms of disgust—an "ick factor" provoked by cultural aesthetic norms for women's bodies. This is most evident in some of the commentary generated by the work, commentary that advises Morris-Cafiero on how to avoid such reactions in others by improving her appearance and losing weight or renders painfully explicit that her body generates "disgust."[13] Once we recognize in ourselves the potential to scorn others' bodies, to root disgust and aversion in aesthetic tastes that differentiate based on internalized, reflexive cultural norms, we are, I think, drawn full circle back to where this chapter began. The body's messages matter and the body's communicative force can foster or undermine sociality with others. These are the stone cold facts about how we work, both physically and psychologically. But to make these facts a force for prosocial good and for humane treatment of individual people entails cultivating humility, guarded by good bodily manners, toward the bodies of others.

Chapter 8

Righteous Incivility Revisited

Where explicit Confucian instruction is concerned, I have reached the end of the road. To follow the Confucian program for improving myself, I should expect that the more attuned I become to my dependencies on others and to my fundamental sociality, the less inclined I will be to disregard the feelings and dignity of others, the less content I will be with tribalized insult or careless affront. The more I practice good manners, the more natural and easy they will become. My internal dispositions will shift under the influence of external behavior to favor more stable appreciation of social bonds and cooperation. As adhering to rules and managing my demeanor become more fluid, I will be less likely to treat others inequitably, ungenerously, or to negatively influence social environments. When all of these pieces come together, I will be, if not good, then better than I am. Such are the convictions embedded in what Confucius and Xunzi offer.

Even as I credit much of what the Confucians offer to be sound and promising, I am nonetheless struck by their almost total silence about what, if anything, might justify incivility and rudeness. Undergirding their counsel is an expectation that my temptations to incivility and rudeness will significantly dissipate as my dispositions shift. This too seems sound and promising, an expectation I can credit as plausible. Yet I cannot believe that *all* temptations to incivility will vanish, nor can I believe that they should. I retain a conviction that surely, some of the time, in some contexts, and with respect to some people, incivility would be justified, perhaps even genuinely *righteous*. I thus find myself at the end of the Confucian road wanting further direction. I still want to know: *when, at long last, may I be rude*? I want, that is, to return to the sorts of temptations I described in chapter 2 and discover what a Confucian-inspired commitment to civility can do to address the sometimes substantial impulse to be "righteously" rude.

Neither Confucius nor Xunzi directly addresses justified incivility, and I must own that I am intrigued by their failure to address a question that, to me, seems inevitable, obvious, and pressing. How could they think so very much and so very hard about civility and yet not answer *this*, not speak to when I might step outside the boundaries and be deliberately rude? One too obvious answer is that they thought I never should, that there is no circumstance that could legitimately invite good, morally significant incivility. To be sure, both Confucius and Xunzi sometimes speak as if *never* deviating from civility and good manners is the only right and proper way, but their blunt, totalizing claims are situated alongside evidence that, in any actual life, it simply won't be so. Confucius himself, lionized as a role model beyond compare, is sometimes *rude*. For example, he once declined to meet a political messenger by claiming illness, but then pointedly, audibly began to play his zither before the messenger could depart.[1] He gave a polite excuse only to deliberately shatter it, announcing its insincerity by vividly exercising his robust good health. That's not just rude, it is exquisitely, deliciously rude.

Given Confucius's thorough mastery of good manners, his occasional departures from civility are doubly noteworthy. They suggest that indeed, one need not *always* be polite and that sometimes being uncivil is in fact good. Presumably, in Confucius's judgment, that messenger or his master *needed* snubbing. Why, then, would neither Confucius nor Xunzi address this explicitly, offer some guidance about when, where, and how incivility can be good? The answer, I think, resides in how difficult it is to say anything that will *help*.

The question—when may I be rude?—has no good and reliable answer, and this has to do with the gap between how the question is framed and what life itself looks like. The question is abstract and general, unmoored from any context, but deciding to be rude is a choice made in a particular context, involving a definite situation full of significant details that will *matter*. To whom would I be rude? About what would I be rude? What is at stake in my rudeness? Who might be influenced, for good or ill, by what I do? These details not only matter, they matter too much to permit any generalized, abstract answer to do the trick and resolve, ahead of time, when rudeness will be judicious and righteous. The general, abstract question has no satisfying answer because the sorts of experiences that would give rise to it—where the question is not theoretical, but immediate and pressing—are simply too complex and too nested in highly particular contexts to allow a formulaic answer or set of principles by which we could make good decisions. Thus, if I am motivated to ask when I may be rude because I expect a tidy formula, I will be, to borrow a lovely Confucian idiom, climbing trees in search of fish.[2]

Where genuinely good and righteous incivilities are concerned, the best I can hope is to develop in myself the best judgment I can and then apply my good judgment in the necessarily seat-of-my-pants contexts life will give me. Of course "develop and exercise good judgment" is the worst sort of command. For it is at once exquisitely sensible and yet utterly elusive. I can credit it as the *right* advice even as I flounder and flail about how to *follow* it. After all, there is a reason etiquette advice columns exist: Sorting out the limits of politeness is *hard* and so we profit from seeing experts in the craft navigate the complications and dilemmas life can inflict on us all. If developing and exercising good judgment were easy, we wouldn't need those advice columns. We can of course try to sort out some more particular guidance by looking at what experts do,[3] seeking to lift out what qualities of understanding and discernment operate in their judgments, but I want instead to come at "good judgment" from the decidedly rattier position I occupy as someone without good judgment but aspiring to better. It seems to me that what I might need to consider will be importantly different from what a sagely figure such as Confucius would. After all, I am likely to make mistakes of a sort Confucius never would.[4] So I want to come at developing better judgment by considering, in my own case, what I think my mistakes are likely to be. If I can identify where I am most prone to error, I can seek to refine my judgment with correctives that will encourage improvement. In this regard, the most basic element in bettering my judgment is treating judicious incivility as *part of* learning to be polite.

Developing good judgment regarding incivility is not a bit of work distinct from all of the other hard work of developing better manners. Rather, good judgment about incivilities will emerge from exactly the processes that yield good manners and civility. Attention to my dependency, sociality, and all of the Big Stuff will pitch me toward the world in ways that will make me less careless in any occasional incivilities, more deliberate in how I encounter others. More specifically, practicing good manners will inculcate skillfulness that profits good judgment. To be well-mannered and civil requires honing attention to exactly the sorts of things that will matter in any effort to be righteously uncivil: being polite entails being socially observant, attentive to other people's standing and sensibilities, astute about the atmospherics of shared spaces and situations, and, most generally, alert to the complexity of social and interactional dynamics. As I become more practiced at all of this, the expectation is that my judgment will improve because it will be rooted in a far more fulsome understanding of context as it informs what will be best and most judicious.

It is likewise important to recognize the substantial role that behavioral habituation and internalization of values will play in my judgment. To recall my earlier analogies, skilled dancers and expert writers achieve a fluidity and naturalness in what they do. They largely follow the rules and practice sound technique, but in doing so, they likewise develop cultivated instincts about the limits of those rules and techniques. One feature of developing skill in dance and grammar is an improved ability to break with sound practice to good effect. In these activities, the better you get, the better your departures from what is usually good and sound will be. Breaches in the ordinary and usual become smarter, more adept, and are used in service to the overall goals in operation; the letter of rule and law is broken precisely to honor its spirit in some way. So too, I expect that long practice with good manners and deep internalization of its values will foster improved judgment about incivilities. Under the power of better acquired instincts and deepened values, one will be more likely to turn one's incivilities toward the spirited purpose of honoring our sociality and dependencies, making incivility work toward the good. Put plainly, then, working on my *good* manners will also work on my *bad*, giving me better judgment about how to use bad manners well and righteously.

Apart from how general training in good manners will conduce to good judgment about when, where, and how to depart from civil conduct, I recognize that my tendencies to make mistakes are themselves not general but reflect what, as Xunzi would say, I am "soaked in." They have a flavor and odor produced by the social and cultural conditions I inhabit. Definite and particular cultural conditions can *discourage* good judgment and influence how errors in judgment will tend. For example, a culture that treasures getting along, not making waves, and assiduously keeping interaction pleasant will discourage incivility even when it would be roundly righteous to let fly with some uncivil dissent. That, of course, is not the culture we inhabit.

My worries are not that I will fail to be rude when I ought to be, but that I will be rude far more often than I should. And this, I think, must be a factor in what improving my judgment will look like, for it inflects what I am really asking when I ask, "When may I be rude?"

For me at least, the question of when I may be rude is largely *about* the world I inhabit. I experience the question's force as a remark on circumstances: I want to know when I may be rude because the social-political world I inhabit seems at present so very divisive, hostile, unpleasant, and ugly. Much of civic life has grown venomous and there are ever fewer spaces uncorrupted by antagonistic and inhumane modes of interaction. I find other people less civil than I once routinely expected and find my own temptations to incivility increasing apace. In Xunzi's idiom, when the horses are neighing hostility and animosity, one does want to neigh right back. Moreover, in a degraded, uncivil public culture, I can be tempted to think civility simply impotent or, worse, a barrier to forcefully dissenting where dissent is needed. On my most cynical days, adhering to standards of civility can feel like carrying a stick to a gunfight, a sure path to defeat in the ever more aggressive contests of values and political life. A distressed desire to be uncivil is thus what most motivates me to ask when I may be uncivil, and the present state of my judgment tilts toward wanting *lots* of permission to be uncivil. Because of this, I want here to focus on two correctives in particular, correctives that answer both to cynicism about what civility can do and to temper impulses coarsened by a culture of aggression and eager pugilism. Let me lead with the first, civility's seeming impotence.

One of the more lamentable developments in contemporary civic life is a propensity to conflate dissent and incivility, to treat dissent *as* incivility and ignore the myriad other forms dissent can take. Many of the commonplace ways of justifying incivility I canvassed in chapter 2 can tilt in this direction, implying that to rudely "speak truth to power" or to baldly "tell it like it is" is what dissenting entails.

At worst, as I suggested, these modes of talk can suggest that there is cowardice or weakness in failing to come out with one's uncivil guns blazing. Yet there is a significant gap between acknowledging that some dissent is uncivil and assuming that dissent *requires* incivility. Much of what dissent can do—contest, dispute, rebuke, admonish, assert alternatives, or even shame—can be done through civil means. Improving my judgment, then, entails entertaining a more expansive understanding of civility than we may be culturally encouraged to see. In this, the Confucians can indeed help. The Confucians were, by painful necessity, adept at civil dissent. They were not, to be sure, always successful—*no* dissent, civil or uncivil, can promise this—but they were clever in how they "spoke truth to power," not least because in their situation, power could kill.

The *Analects* records a couple of examples of Confucius engaging with Ji Kangzi, a warlord both ambitious and corrupt. Xunzi once compared interacting with a violent lord who is unworthy of respect as engaging with a tiger,[5] and this is just what Confucius appears to be doing in these passages. In them, Ji is ostensibly seeking Confucius's advice, but his queries also appear ironic. Indeed, he appears to be baiting Confucius, soliciting advice he has no intention of taking and flexing his power to aggravate and insult. In one passage, Ji asks Confucius what to do about bandits and Confucius replies, "If you yourself were truly not covetous, though you rewarded people for it, they would not steal."[6] A second interaction features Ji lightly toying with a plan to execute any who depart from the good. Executing wrongdoers, he offers, is doubly useful, for it would eliminate those on the wrong track while providing a forceful incentive for others to stay on it. Confucius's responds by remarking a far easier solution: "If you desire goodness, the people will be good."[7] He then elaborates by noting the good ruler's power to bend people toward the good as wind bends the grass. This second exchange is of course especially fraught. It is impossible to know whether Ji intended his question as a threat, but it surely does advertise Ji's raw power and his inclinations to use it.

Confucius's responses to Ji offer a style of dissent that is simultaneously civil and extraordinarily damning. In each, Confucius utilizes what were then commonplace claims about how a ruler can steer others by example. Indeed, the claims are rather banal, but therein resides much of their power. Faced with a menacing warlord, Confucius renders him implicitly weak, a "ruler" in need of remedial insight any effective ruler would already apprehend. Confucius rebukes and remonstrates, gamely operating as if Ji's questions are sincere but offering advice that inverts Ji's power: if you were a better person and ruler, Confucius suggests, these problems would have solved themselves already. Confucius thereby asserts a bit of his own power, an authority to think ill of Ji and locate his troubles in his own failures. Confucius's remarks are, in sum, potent stuff and rendered all the more potent for their unflinching, cool civility. Confucius rebukes and indeed shames—that is, he achieves one of the purposes we imagine righteous incivility to have—but does so absent recourse to open, explicit disrespect.

Confucius's encounters with a tiger suggest that even great provocation can be met with civil dissent, but given the power dynamic in play, they may be of limited use. Perhaps all of us would be compelled to better judgment in civilly pitching our dissent if we were faced with violent warlords. And, indeed, being clever about keeping dissent civil is an art historically cultivated most by those who lack power. Even so, Confucius's example does at least usefully inspire me to recognize how keeping dissent civil is often a matter of *imagination*, of obliging myself to seek ways of expressing opposition that stay in bounds even as they do what dissent does. And we do not need to look to Confucius for this, but have more recent examples.

During the US Democratic convention of 2016, Michelle Obama gave a speech in which she famously proclaimed: "When they go low, we go high."[8] The claim was at once a rebuke and a statement of aspiration, a condemnation of uncivil discourse and a statement of resolve to avoid it. It was, in several respects, a masterpiece of dissent civilly delivered. With it, Obama repudiated as "low" a politics of insult and derision, disagreeing with her political opponents while publicly committing herself to foreswear insult and derision. She thus effectively made the civil *form* of her disagreement a substantive element in disagreement itself. Should she indeed live up to the aspirational elements of this claim in future, her every civil gesture in answer to incivilities becomes inflected with the power of protest: the resolve to be civil come what may can itself be a form of protest and, significantly, a source of considerable political potency. Should she instead sometimes abandon her resolve and be uncivil, her incivility will likely have a power that the habitually uncivil never achieve. One marked advantage of habitual civility is that it makes one's rare incivility really count in a calculus of effective dissent.

Apart from how power may accrue to the civil dissenter, such a strategy can also encourage others to greater civility—indeed, sometimes it may *compel* civility by making incivility seem far worse than it otherwise would. Upon hearing Obama's speech, I spared a pitying thought for any subsequent convention speakers who opted to "go low," for Obama had effectively reframed how those speakers would be heard. They would not only appear "low," any sense that theirs could be a *necessary* righteous incivility had been undercut by the shaming dignity of Obama's remarks. Civil dissent can direct how others' incivility will be heard and interpreted. That civil dissent can frame the uncivil in unappealing ways can be a source of considerable power—at the very least, it can relieve any worries that civility is the proverbial stick at a gunfight. At my most fanciful, I imagine strategies such as Confucius's and Obama's to be cases in which civility itself gets weaponized. Aspects of the 1960s civil rights movement in the United States abundantly demonstrate the logic in play here.

Suffering even great abuse without answering in kind can cast an abusive climate into ever-sharper relief. In this way, civil dissent may not only be weaponized, it can disarm. It can reduce the power of one's opponent by exposing the opponent's degradation, his easy contentment with the ignoble, his lack of limit and restraint. The opponent's incivility becomes a weapon that is turned on himself in any contest for public sympathy and esteem. In this regard, I must admit, the "good judgment" I seek to cultivate includes a desire to be crafty and cunning, to stay civil not (just) because it is more humane, but also because it can be so formidable, so very hardcore.

I realize of course that much of what I say about the power of civil dissent coupled with my use of violent metaphor puts me in an odd spot with much of what I have said in this book. Having argued against reflexive tribalism and in favor of humility before one's opponents, having critiqued celebrations of pugilistic "righteous incivility," I am now cutting loose with rather cynical suggestions about how I might *weaponize* my civility and, let's face it, cleverly shame those who disagree with me. Even as I see this tension, I think it vitally important to emphasize a truth too often obscured in our contemporary climate: that civility *can* be sharp, forceful, and pointed. This is a truth sometimes acknowledged by people such as myself, reared in the southern United States, where civil forms of devastating rebuke are part of the local idiom. "Bless your heart" can mean just that, but it can also mean "Damn you to hell and your kin along with you." Making clever use of the subtle, the indirect, and even the ambiguous *can* "speak truth to power"— after all, Confucius effectively blesses Ji Kangzi's heart. Civility lacks the heat of insult, derision, and affront, but it is a mistake to overlook its cool power. And to be sure, wanting power is often a factor in wanting to be uncivil.

Too often, we speak as if the incentives to incivility rest in incivility's *power*, as if the *reason* to be uncivil is to wrest power from a world that would deny it to you. My aim in emphasizing how civility may be weaponized is thus meant as a corrective for just this, to acknowledge the failures in imagination that would have me see incivility as the most powerful or, worse, *only* route to forceful dissent. Once I recognize that civil dissent is not only possible, but can be radically potent, I will be less prone to the mistaken and crude equation of incivility and dissent. In our current political climate, it is not obvious to me that incivility does enjoy more potency than civility. Where incivility is freely, excessively used, civil rebuke and dissent becomes all the more noteworthy and, if one of the aims of dissent is to summon attention to social wrongs and ills, civility may be more effective for its rarity. This was likely one reason Obama's convention comments drew the widespread notice that they did.

If part of good judgment entails recognizing the potential power of keeping dissent and disagreement civil, it is only a part. We need to be more imaginative about strategies for disagreeing with others and dissenting against conditions we find morally repugnant, but this aspect of good judgment has a decidedly cynical cast. It doesn't do to overcorrect and treat civil dissent as but guerilla-style tactics. What of the more optimistic elements of good manners that infuse the Confucian account of them? What of our aspirations to flourishing forms of human dependency and sociality? These aspirations are foundationally important in motivating good manners, but can they introduce correctives to judgment where our relations with others are fractured by division, disagreement, and alienation born of deep conflict? Correctives rooted in optimistic aspirations regarding our sociality are, I admit, the most difficult to achieve. Regrettably, I think them also the most necessary where developing better judgment in our current climate is concerned. The trick is how to keep our optimistic aspirations well grounded in a world where too much optimism could make us civil in ways violate much that is right, good, and noble.

It is good to want flourishing shared humanity, but surely not at any cost, not against *every* provocation others may offer. As nebulous and elusive as "good judgment" is, we want it to include *both* our prosocial desires for shared humanity *and* our own good moral sense. And of course it is the latter, our own good moral sense, that often inspires impulses to incivility: incivility can seem necessary if I am to oppose views or behaviors I judge to threaten what is good, noble, or right. Moreover, for most of us, what we judge "good, noble, and right" will be firmly *attached to* our prosocial commitments. Uncivilly repudiating a person employing a racist epithet, for example, may sacrifice my chances of establishing shared accord with him, but the "good, noble, and right" I thereby defend has much to do with shared humanity: in such cases, uncivil rebuke of one can constitute just defense of others and of wider humanity. Such is to say that human solidarity is a tricky business that resolute, infallibly civil interaction cannot by itself achieve.

Any aspiration for a totalizing solidarity with *all* has to answer to the regrettable reality that solidarity with some can undermine solidarity with others. Sometimes we do indeed have to choose where we will express our solidarity and efforts to keep civil sociality with everyone will be morally damaging. This dynamic is, I expect, painfully familiar, as it features in one of the more perennial tropes in current popular dialogues about manners: what to do at a family dinner when Uncle Frank is offensively opining about "the blacks," "the gays," "the illegal immigrants," "the Muslims," or about any social demographic group presently stimulating his considerable and belligerent biases. The trouble Uncle Frank poses is that he creates conditions where civil responses to him appear to sacrifice the dignity, worth, and humanity of other people. More broadly, one of the more compelling provocations to incivility is surely just when the uncivil response works to affirm shared humanity against any who might undermine it, when dealing an uncivil blow to one strikes a greater blow for our aspirations for all. Reasoning such as this is of course among the temptations to righteous incivility I detailed in chapter 2, but let me return to this theme and consider how judgment better informed by a Confucian-inspired sociality might feature in how such temptations can be met.

I have already made plain that I have deep doubts about how righteous incivility is popularly described. I am skeptical of the heroic narratives of gadflies and iconclasts who "call it like they see it" where the errors of others are concerned, of the arrogance bluntly "speaking truth to power" can promote, and, most fundamentally, of the ways we cast the righteously uncivil as those who eagerly stand apart from the herd and critique. I have little patience with valorizing the practice of uncivilly "calling out" every Uncle Frank the world includes. The risks here are several, but notably include our tendencies to reflexively position ourselves as morally superior to those we would critique, to be hasty in our evaluations of others and of just who deserves uncivil critique, and the fracturing, tribalizing effects of writing off sociality with those who disagree with us. There is, in short, a psychology that can accompany free use of righteous incivility that is at odds with the deep sociality and dependency the Confucians recommend we cultivate. And it is a deeply *tempting* psychology precisely because it can seem to free me from *them*, from *those people* who reject my views and values. These concerns provoke in me a desire for an alternative psychology of disagreement, for bettered judgment about how to disagree without thereby severing myself from others. I think some of what this will entail is already familiar to many of us. Let me explain by way of an example.

Not long ago, one of my students brought in a "civility dilemma" for class discussion. He had been home from college visiting his beloved grandparents, elders with whom he had a young lifetime filled with rich, nurturing, and loving experiences. While visiting, he attended church with them only to find their preacher avowing in the sermon views that my student counted morally repulsive, hateful, and in violation of his own deeply held convictions. It was, in short, just the sort of sermon Uncle Frank himself would deliver. My student's dilemma, upon hearing the sermon was just this: he wanted to rise from his seat and depart in disgust, to register his disagreement and revulsion with his feet and demeanor. But he found himself torn precisely because he was there with his grandparents. He understood that any protest gesture he made would wound them. It would embarrass them before their community and rupture the gentle give and take of their relation to him. My student and his grandparents disagreed about many things, but habitually took care in how they disagreed, engaging with consideration and respect whatever their deep differences. This, then, was my student's dilemma: get up and leave in protest, or stay in place as if he agreed with what the preacher was saying? He was torn about what to do, unhappily conflicted and unsure. Such feelings of disorientation and uncertainty are, I think, responses we would do well to cultivate in ourselves, for they represent an attitude toward disagreement that is at once harder to endure yet more commendable in its prosocial orientation.[9]

My student's struggle consisted most fundamentally in dual attachments, attachment to his circumspect moral commitments and attachment to his grandparents. The dilemma pinched precisely because neither of these are trivial attachments—they are instead the stuff of life-governing importance, the stuff that he perceived as making him the person that he is. No matter what he did, then, he was going to feel terrible about it, was going to feel that he had sacrificed something, whether it be accord with his grandparents or his sense of wider human dignity and what he judged noble, good, and right. The psychological orientation toward disagreement in play here is especially striking in how it departs from our popular models of "heroic" righteous incivility. Let me make this contrast a bit more explicit.

The "heroically" uncivil person our popular rhetoric describes tends to be triumphal. He finds another's judgment or behavior wrong and so bravely "calls out" error in a way that sets him and his individual moral judgment apart. Yet, as my student's example attests, there are other, more richly relational ways that other people's wrongness can experientially register. In recognizing that another person or even my community writ large is significantly, importantly wrong, I may be disappointed, disenchanted, or heartbroken. I can, that is, experience the break between my own good moral sense and that of my community as sorrowful, as opening up an alienation from others in a way that I deeply regret and would powerfully wish to have otherwise. I want my community *not* to be wrong and resolving that they are is thus painful. There is no triumph in one's own rightness and others' wrongness, no smug delight in delivering a "sick burn" of incivility that would humiliate or shame. When relational connection and attachment to others is salient, conflict is internal as well as external. One disagrees with others, but one is also internally torn about just how to manage this in light of the multiple pulls of one's attachments. As painful as such conflicting pulls may be, the discomfort of the experience is rooted in some of our most salutary and noble impulses: the desire for others to be their best selves and a related longing to cleanly admire them. Put plainly, even as they mess up, we want to *like* and morally *esteem* those we love.

Our narratives regarding heroic incivility rarely acknowledge the painful estrangement, internal conflict, and, most foundationally, desire to esteem others that grounded my student's dilemma. Rather, our heroic models of incivility emphasize instead the uncivil person's high confidence, a bold willingness to forcefully avow disagreement however much it may displease others. Significantly, this was a posture my student indirectly acknowledged as he analyzed the nature of his dilemma. Had he encountered the views he heard in his grandparents' church expressed elsewhere in the world and by strangers to whom he felt no ties, he avowed, he would have freely let fly with a hostile, insulting, dismissive response. He would have rebuked with the full force of his outrage. There would be no check, hesitation, or tempering, only incivility. For he could easily write off a stranger as one of *those people*. With his grandparents, the trouble was that *my people* and *those people* were collapsing together: those people *were* his people. Because he knew them, he felt he could and ought expect better of them and that he could and ought try to bring them toward better, an effort he could only undertake if he did not consign them to the ash heap of *those people*—that is, if he did not treat their concerns, feelings, and interests as irrelevant in how he formulated his own reactions. Most significantly, because he did care for his grandparents and know them well, he could not treat disagreement with them as totalizing.

It is easiest to repudiate others as *those people* when we know little about them. With strangers or more distant acquaintances, disagreement can swamp everything else we might otherwise notice about them. Disagreement can readily become all that we see and understand of another person: lacking any substantial knowledge of another's history, personality, or wider values and absent any context of relation to them, a comparative stranger who disagrees with me can readily register less as a person than an idea. As I suggested in chapter 5, we may carry around a host of assumptions about what *kind* of person holds what *kinds* of views and values or even trivial preferences; we expect certain *types* of views to belong to certain *types* of people. Because of this, when I interact with those I know little or not at all, I can feel like I disagree with the whole person, not just one of his views, actions, or preferences. Rather than see any disagreement in the discrete form it manifests, the impulse is to see my opponent as a symbolic manifestation of *all* I implicitly associate with the view he holds. In contexts like our own, where political and civic discord run high, the worry is that this impulse leaves us all battling caricatures. Discrete disagreements become total and the other becomes an enemy because we substitute cynical assumptions about his character for more personal knowledge, conscripting him to represent All That Is Wrong with the World. And once we have vaulted well past discrete disagreement and drafted someone to stand for All That Is Wrong With the World, uncivilly *punching* starts to seem like a pretty good plan.

We clearly cannot expect to get to know all of the others with whom we disagree, nor, let's face it, would we want to do so. Yet where we do not know others, we can nonetheless adjust and modulate what we do in our ignorance. Rather than substitute dark assumptions about another's character, we can supplement our interpretations of him with something like the generosity and indeed heartbreak we extend in deep disagreement with those we love, we can try to be *torn* about how to interact.

Even the most uncivil among us will yet have relationships in which the quick uncivil impulse is checked, slowed, or tempered. The prospect of hurting or offending those we care about makes incivility less compelling, more fraught and troubling. So perhaps the trick in better regulating wider impulses to incivility rests in just such relationships, in borrowing the internal conflict these relationships can produce and applying it elsewhere, with more distant others. We can incorporate some of what produces internal conflict in managing disagreement with friends into our dealings with others to whom we have fewer, or even no, relational bonds. The checks, pauses, and tempering elements producing internal conflict may include, for example, humility in judgments about others, a desire to think better of others than their views may immediately suggest possible, a resolution to try persuasion (even prolonged persuasion) in a self-consciously strategic optimism about others, a sense of social responsibility to engage others for better even where engaging will be painful, or a determination to navigate dispute humanely in compassion for others' sense of social face or dignity. These are all the sort of things at work in making my student's experience register as a *dilemma* rather than merely an invitation to discourtesy. And they are, more generally, the strategies that can slow down hasty impulses to uncivilly deride, scorn, or wholly write off others with whom we disagree. Most importantly, they keep in view the long goal: developing ever more robust and flourishing forms of dependency and sociality.

Ultimately, even as I consider ways that civility can operate fiercely in contests of public values, my better aspirations are not about weaponizing civility in combat with others, but about finding routes to armistice. I don't really want whatever private satisfactions might come from being right or the triumphs of "my side" defeating yours. To be sure, there may be situations in which what the entire world needs most is for Uncle Frank just to shut up. But where our aims are steered by longings for community and robust, thriving dependencies, we will not want to tell him so too soon, before we try to engage, to understand, and to keep him as one of those we count *ours*. To the extent that I think my own views right, noble, and good, I will want them widely shared, not simply the prevailing force in a social dominance exercise that quiets opposition. More importantly, pursuit of values that are indeed right, noble, and good is a task that *needs* others. As Cheshire Calhoun argues, we should not make the mistake of thinking that "morality is first and foremost about 'getting it right' as individuals."[10] Rather, "morality is also something we do together." Because we do depend upon each other and because we are deeply, ineluctably social creatures, we need to reason together. And reasoning together profits from strategic optimism, from resolute longings to be well-disposed toward others even where, and perhaps *especially* where, it is most difficult.

The peril, as I see it, is that if I am going to be wiser about my uncivil impulses, I need to shift my judgment away from all-too-easy "heroics" against others I am too eagerly pitched to dislike. This, combined with recognizing the potential power of civil responses, especially in contexts fraught by incivility or worse, can work to keep my righteous incivilities rare and, most importantly, will lend them a different character. Perhaps the most fundamental shift achieved by working on manners and civility is to introduce tensions into experiences that presently seem easy. To be sure, working on my good manners will make it easier and less effortful to be polite, but it will also render impulses to rudeness harder and more difficult to navigate. For the values informing my practice of good manners will make me more reluctant to engage in "heroic" displays of disrespect for those who disagree with me, less prone to reach for the satisfactions of being "right" and rudely deriding the "wrong." In good judgment, I want strategies for standing with, rather than apart from, my social partners and society. This is of course not always possible—sometimes we find ourselves exiled from others against our will and better intentions, against even our most defiant optimism. Likewise, sometimes incivility will be the best course but, significantly, it will be tinged with regret and distress.

The more I internalize the dependencies and sociality that bind me to others, the more painful alienation and from others will seem. Incivility, under the auspices of the Big Stuff, the values infusing the Confucian commitment to manners, represents a break in our bonds with others and a break in our ability to be bonded with them. Incivility effectively announces: I just can't do it; I cannot keep our bond intact and unruptured. It thereby remarks realities we would, as social creatures, powerfully wish otherwise. Notably, understanding this may make us more compassionate in witnessing incivility in others. Indeed, we may come to see others' incivilities as markers of distress and suffering, and this, in turn, will decrease the temptation to answer in kind every hostile "neigh" I hear from others. Where my own incivilities are concerned, however, I want to regret them. I want them, in other words, to register how my commitments to the Big

Stuff transform the triumphal "heroics" our culture encourages into disappointment and sorrow.

Bettering my judgment about righteous incivilities will have the consequence of leaving me more often torn in how I encounter dispute and disagreement. Indeed, I will be trying to make myself feel torn in this way more often. And taking this approach won't make life any easier when I do disagree with those around me, for it will often entail maintaining interaction with people I could otherwise dismiss. Not letting fly with an uncivil rebuke also means I cannot as readily fly from such encounters—to stay civil is, more often, to *stay engaged*. By trying to be well-disposed toward others, I try to preserve social connection, even when doing so is displeasing, alienating, and terrible. The defiant optimism underwriting this resolve would have me hold out hope that we will all be better for making such efforts, that we can find some fellow feeling, some scrap of shared humanity that will enable better (or at least not worse) forms of shared life. However attractive the aims in all of this, though, it must be said that there is much here that will be experientially unpleasant. And this, in turn, invites me to consider the wider felt qualities of a polite life: to ask, what can I expect it to be like to live politely? Should I aspire to a life that conceives thriving as thriving with and among other people, how will this influence the quality my own life has?

Chapter 9

Disappointments and Consolation

Any time we undertake a change in how our lives are structured, it is
helpful to have a sense of what change will yield. This is a significant
factor in making a change, for imagination about what will come next,
what will flow from alteration, is a substantial element in maintaining
the motivation required to persist in the work that change entails. The
hope of course is that changes will be improvements in the quality
of one's life, one's relationships, and one's society. Where cultivating
better manners is concerned, the hope is that I will enjoy more fruitful and enlivening relations with others, that I will find my sociality
more richly rewarding and be a better friend, companion, and citizen.
I would hope that being more polite will not simply make *me* better,
but make my *life* better, offering new or newly increased forms of satisfaction, relation, and, most broadly, distinctively socially enriched
forms of happiness and well-being.

In my efforts to make use of what the Confucians have to say
about good manners and civility, I am driven less by a conviction that
they are right to think our sociality the fundament of what we are
than by a sense that I want it to be so. This too seems one of those
pliable aspects of humanity, a reality that is negotiable, not fixed,
and dependent on how I conduct my relations with others. That
is, without any ambitious or final philosophical conclusions about
what human beings really are, I can choose to live as if relations with

others and meaningful sociality are where my life finds its richest blessings and purpose. In this, I am as moved as Confucius appears to be by the gentle pleasures of friendship, of meaningful efforts to make a shared world better through my efforts, and of the rewarding appreciation that comes from recognizing how deeply woven my well-being is with that of others. I find living such a life appealing, and I am attracted by the thought that living as if it is so may make it so, or at least closer to so. I am willing, that is, to summon up precursive faith as best I can. But I must also allow that my always-tenuous faith is often tested, often betrayed by a social world that tempts me to succumb to alienation, despair, and misanthropy. I suffer from considerable inconstancy, great doubts that I really can keep the faith.

So I am left with one last bit of reflection, an effort to discover what there is to carry one through when faith is lost, when one longs to disentangle oneself from humanity and leave the fray to those at ease with the inhumane hostility and uncivil combat that increasingly defines it. Indeed, while I am sometimes tempted to be rude and uncivil, the greater temptation is to let go caring what the world is like beyond the narrow confines of those about whom I can most natively and easily care. This is not, or at least not primarily, a desire to abide with *my people* and let the rest do as they will. Rather, it concerns the broadest affirmative ambitions of the Confucian project, the resolution to stay in the mix, to keep prizing one's sociality and dependency even when doing so seems to yield few good results or, even worse, is simply punishing. At issue in such a temptation is a variation on one of the more fundamental quandaries in ethics: why seek to be good? More elaborately, why seek to be good when doing so entails great struggle and can sometimes seem so damnably discouraging? Where politeness in particular is concerned, why adopt the strategic aspiration to bind myself to others and hitch my well-being to relations in a social world I often find unhappy, unpleasant, and alienating?

These questions, I fear, can sometimes invite cheap and easy philosophical answers. They concern both what can motivate us to do good and what we can expect of our lives when we try to do good. There is something in the human being—or at least in me—that wants good effort to be answered with good result, that wants being good to work out well for the one being good. So when I seek to frame my expectations of what living a polite life will yield, I recognize an impulse to reach for heartily pleasing possibilities, ways to give this story a happy ending. I might, for example, appeal to the ennobling rewards of making the world a better place. In being polite, I will, as the Confucians suggest, steer others, the breeze of my civility tilting the grass of others' conduct toward greater kindness and generosity. I will thus not only cease to inflict harms on others, I will contribute to a world in which such harms are reduced. So too, I might appeal to the intrinsic rewards of improving myself. Being good can feel quite good and virtue, so the saying goes, is its own reward. For it enables a form of self-esteem grounded in values I can circumspectly prize. In sum, I might say that living a polite life will yield formidably important life satisfactions, both external and internal. It would redeem all the struggles of being civil with the grand promise that I will make the world better and that I will find exalted personal satisfactions doing so. This would indeed be heady stuff. Alas, it also sounds utterly naive. Such ambitious consolations cannot carry me through the difficult and punishing aspects of being polite for the simple reason that I cannot believe them.

Regrettably, being polite does not inevitably, reliably steer others to follow suit. Nor does being polite transform the world, even when it does help some. Part of what motivates my interest in being more civil is that I *feel* the distress of my society being riven by conflict, aggression, and division. But even as the intensity of this distress does some motivational work, making me more interested in changing myself, it also makes me less likely to credit any strongly optimistic claims about what my own improvement can do. Put plainly, the trouble here is big and I am small. Expectations that I can, by my own efforts, work a change in wider social conditions will, in the long run, be self-defeating. When the world defies my good efforts, as it surely will, giving up will be compelling. If I am motivated by high aspirations to make a big difference, the inevitable failures in achieving this payoff will be demotivating, so best not to imagine that being polite will yield a life rendered better because the world itself will become markedly better.

Equally regrettable, being good is not reliably intrinsically rewarding. Indeed, when I mentally canvass examples of people I admire for their goodness, I cannot help but notice how truly awful their lives can sometimes seem. Being good does not reliably make one's life good, at least not "good" in the ordinary ways.[1] Many who do good actively suffer for it, experiencing hardships and heartbreak they would not were they *less* committed to being good. From humanitarian aid workers in war zones to jailed rights activists to the myriad quiet moral volunteers who heroically try to improve their communities, suffering is a familiar companion, an ineluctable part of what they do. To be sure, there may exist some rare human creatures who draw all of their life satisfaction from doing good even as it reduces their immediate satisfactions and comfort, but I am not one. For myself, I find the internal rewards of virtue altogether too spare and mean to compensate for all of the suffering and heartbreak doing good can engender. Whatever private, internal satisfactions may derive from being good, I simply can't find them all that great.

Because I cannot credit grand promises of great rewards for being good, I find that the questions about motivations and consolations I bring to being polite have a darker cast. For they are premised on strong doubts that being polite *will* significantly make either my world or my life better, that the considerable effort entailed trying to be more polite will *matter*. Thus, I do not really ask: Why be polite?

Rather, I ask: Why be polite when the rewards of it may be few, when one cannot count on any of the good effects, both personal and relational, politeness ought bring? When resolute efforts to be polite seem to make *no substantial difference*, why keep at it? How can one *keep trying* even as the world defies your best efforts and stubbornly abides in its contentious, brutalizing discord? And, most emphatically, what ought I make of what I *lose* in being polite, of the fact that being civil may not only fail to reward but may sacrifice some of the comforts I currently enjoy? Being civil, put plainly, costs me something.

By adopting a resolve to be well-disposed toward others, I will lose any ease in other, often more comfortable dispositions, the ones that too readily pitch me against thinking well of others. Whatever compensations and consolations a polite life might offer, they need to address how the prosocial dispositions underwriting good manners truncate or wholly cut off other dispositions, dispositions that can provide a sort of experiential comfort. These losses include having far less recourse to cynicism that would pitch me to expect the worst of others, to detachment that would render me indifferent to how my relations with others proceed, or to outrage that would greet the poor conduct of others with swift and dismissive condemnation. While these superficially represent unpleasant ways to feel and to orient myself toward others, they do, perversely, afford considerable comfort in an age of strife and contention. They can at least make unpleasant experience a little less so.

When I am cynical about what others are like or what they may do, I am at least unsurprised when they are terrible, buffered against unpleasant shock. Others behaving badly will not betray my cynical expectations but merely fulfill them, and even the cold comfort of finding low expectations met is a comfort of sorts. When I am detached from others, psychologically unmoored from my sociality with them, what they do will not matter much to me. Their conduct simply will not bear on my well-being or contentment, and this too affords a certain protection, a way to stand free of what is ugly or unlovely in others. Outrage might at first blush seem an irredeemably unpleasant state, but it can be distinctively purifying. At the very least, expressed outrage can separate me from any whose views I abhor, letting me be *done with them* and indeed done with all this effortful nicety about "reasoning together." In this way, outrage can feel like a spa day, an opportunity both to expel toxins and to retreat from the labor of being polite. In short, cynicism, detachment, and outrage can be a relief. But they are forms of relief largely lost to me as I try to be more polite. For each entails sacrificing the optimism upon which good manners must run.

Whether I adopt Confucius's aspirational model emphasizing the potential beauty of our sociality or take on Xunzi's self-consciously strategic model emphasizing the power of manners to avoid misanthropy, I will need hope. To be well-disposed toward others as manners requires, I will need to trust, or at least to appear to trust, better from others than they may deal me. Relative to cynicism, detachment, or outrage, optimism can leave one comparably unprotected and vulnerable. Being polite can feel like extending a hand to another only to find one's hand rebuffed or, worse, slapped away. So too, sometimes one extends that hand through great force of will, when one would rather shake a fist, so the failure to find an answering, kindred response not only thwarts the civil gesture, it insults the effort. Being polite can entail significant vulnerability, its more generous gestures a way of saying, "I want to think well of you." So when it is answered with rudeness, the effect is akin to being sucker punched. One is left unguarded, exposed, and one's opponent sees his advantage and takes it. Optimistic hope, put plainly, can fail and fail spectacularly. Such outcomes are *part of* living politely. And what they illuminate for me is a hidden requirement of trying to be more well-mannered. If I am to pitch myself toward the world in hope, I will need to get quite good at being disappointed.

Unlike cynicism, detachment, or outrage, disappointment yields little I can cast as comfort, for disappointment attaches to longings that are unmet and unfulfilled. The Confucian model of good manners encourages me to want much I may not win. I am to want an expansive social well-being that encompasses not merely my own individual satisfactions, but satisfactions I can only gain with others. In some respects, I need no encouragement to want this. For where the people I love are concerned, I cannot separate my doing well from theirs or, more potently, I care not for flourishing that would be mine alone if those I love did not also, and with me, flourish. I expect I am like most in this. The Confucian model of sociality invites me to a life in which these more native longings are broadened and bolder, encouraging a desire to see the entire social world as part of what makes my life go well and meaningfully for me. Yet the more I cultivate this desire, the more I court disappointment. And the more I recognize how hard optimism truly is.

The sort of optimism good manners entails is doubly hard, both difficult to maintain and muscular. It requires resisting easy comforts and suffering disappointments without succumbing to total defeat. It will entail a resolve not to be done with *them*, with those who defy my efforts for better, but to aim for socially shared progress while soaked in division and hostility. So too, it requires not purification, but getting dirty. To insistently act on optimistic longings is to stay in the mess, engaging with views I despise, aiming for generosity with those I cannot (yet) like, and entertaining dialogue that may leave me feeling sullied. Rather than cleanly repudiate, I negotiate, navigate, and attempt to reason respectfully. While good manners and civility are sometimes derided as prim and prissy, here they require getting one's hands dirty, forgoing the purifying effects of a severing outrage in order to stay attached in all the muck and mess, treating oneself as bound in sociality even to those one would rather despise. And this, to be sure, is also disappointing. For even as I long for the beauty of thriving sociality, the longing itself will hold me in the mire. Being civil, that is, courts the discrete disappointments of encounters with others that go badly no matter my efforts and it also courts existential disappointments. What I *want* will place me more deeply in what I do *not* want; the price of longing for a better world is to make me more fully occupy the world I in fact have, feeling all its pains and alienations.

In seeking consolations for the struggles of living politely, then, I find myself instead with more work to hand, in need of ways to get good at enduring disappointment. What might it mean to be good at *this*? Where being polite is concerned, I think there is at least some low-hanging fruit, ways to think about what to avoid when disappointed. Disappointment, after all, can render us mean, invite resentment, and tempt the comforts of cynicism, detachment, or outrage. I recognize in my own conduct how corrupting disappointment can be, as one ugly social encounter can leave me lashing out or ungenerous in others; disappointed with one, I can turn harsh with many others. At an everyday level, then, part of being good at disappointment is simply containing it, refusing to let discrete frustrations become more diffuse and general. This is sensible and prudent, but I want to dwell on the deeper disappointment embedded in a life of manners, the ways that pursuing good manners will often entail persisting with longings for what one simply cannot have. For I suspect that managing this far less tractable and far more global disappointment is key to life's smaller, daily disappointments. On this score, I find the example of Confucius compelling.

One of the qualities I most admire in Confucius is how palpably he sometimes wanted to give up. It is this that reassures me that however unlike we are—him with his impeccably well-ordered internal life and me with my ratty mixed motives and chaotic impulses—he does get that none of this is easy. He gets that all the trying can be dispiriting, that the outcomes one wants and the outcomes one gets are too often tragically far apart, and that, because of this, one wants just to flee it all, to give up all the effort and just recede into whatever mode of life best promises escape from the world as it is.

One of my favorite passages in the *Analects* is a dialogue between Confucius and his students, young men who, like Confucius, were perennially seeking employment as political advisors.[2] In it, Confucius asks each what he would do if he were at last free to influence state affairs—that is, he asks what they would do with power if they had it and could really begin to make a difference. The first students to answer describe ambitions clearly forged in political and social turmoil. One wants to eliminate famine and protect a vulnerable state from its more powerful, aggressive neighbors. Another wants to address the persistent material deprivation of the common people and ensure their basic needs are met. A third more modestly imagines he could be a minor official charged with restoring court ceremony. The last, Zeng Xi, says that what he most wants is to go to the River Yi with friends. There they would swim, feel the wind on their skin, and, finally, return home singing. On hearing this, Confucius sighs deeply and says simply, "I'm with Zeng Xi."

All of Confucius's students, except Zeng Xi, express the sorts of desires they are supposed to have, the sorts of ambitions and aspirations that commend them as people invested in making the world better. But the dialogue swerves off in an intriguing direction with Zeng Xi's comment and, especially, Confucius's sighing, wistful agreement with him. I don't think Zeng Xi really rejects the sorts of aspirations his peers avow, nor of course does Confucius. After all, if they had earnestly wished it, both Zeng Xi and Confucius could have abandoned political life and just retreated to swimming with friends. Indeed, there are potent philosophical writings in early China that encourage people to do just this: Reject the perilous turmoil of political involvement and instead seek your own private happiness and well-being.[3] Neither Zeng Xi nor Confucius did this, but what registers potently in this exchange is that they *wanted to*. They knew disappointment and felt keenly what keeping hope denied them.

Confucius never did get a world of swimming and singing with friends. Instead, he spent his life struggling mightily for the sorts of goals his other students avowed, trying to influence his world toward better. When he says his wishes align with Zeng Xi's, he indirectly confesses that life as he actually lives it is rather exhausting and dispiriting. Instead of singing with friends on a fine spring day, he spent his days struggling to influence people he could neither like nor admire and with whom he most often did not succeed. In doing so, he relinquished a life he might have had, one cossetted in the comforts of friends and like-minded companions. And he took up a life of hope that would, in his lifetime, pass unfulfilled. He persisted in disappointment in place of contentment, struggle in place of ease, and held to the harder longing that all this sacrifice might somehow matter. So what, then, kept it all going for him?

My own sense is that Confucius's life was not powered by the grand promises. His was not a life in which virtue itself was all the reward he desired, nor did he see the ambitious good effects at which his considerable efforts aimed. Instead, I tend to see his life as powered by something far more modest, something like this: do the best you can, and hope for the best you can, with the circumstances life gives you. This is a far more modest variation on the grand promises and, significantly, takes account of the fact that we will live in the world as we find it. What we get to make of ourselves and how our lives will go is set into conditions we largely do not get to choose. When the world as we find it is bad and inhospitable to our longings, we can try to shift it, even where any success in this is likely to be modest, delayed, and incomplete. The consolation here might just be the humble satisfaction of recognizing that what I cannot like I have sought to change. There have in fact been many in the world who operate this way. One example is "craggy-faced" Bill Bailey, a World War II veteran quoted in Studs Terkel's oral history of the war.[4]

Terkel's history of the war compiles the testimony of many ordinary people who, we might say, wanted to swim with friends but instead found themselves drafted into lives they never imagined for themselves and would not have chosen. But Bailey's account of how he thought of it all is especially striking. Bailey says, in recalling his experience in the war:

> I still think we're all part of somethin', call it the history of the human race, if you want to. I feel that if some guy ten years from now has got some halfway decent conditions, I wanna feel that I helped in some small way to make it possible for him to enjoy them conditions. I mean, that's the name of the game. I just want somebody to say, Them poor son-of-a-bitches, they musta taken a beating back in the old days. We don't know all the names, but glory to them, or somethin' like that.[5]

What Bailey articulates so well is how sometimes the plan we would like for our lives instead becomes abducted by events. Even as one wants the world to be better than it is—to *enjoy* a life in a better world—one gets the world one gets. Then one can, as Bailey does and as Confucius did, become one of those "poor son-of-a-bitches" who gets a "beating" in the always-fragile hope that doing so may make something better, someday, for someone. Figures like Confucius and Baily give up swimming and swallow disappointment, while keeping the longing that gave rise to it. They want their own lives to be more rewarding and pleasing than they are, but disappointment is framed in the wider world in which it occurs. Carefree swimming with friends could not be won by ignoring the cares of the world. It would indeed be nice not to care. But it would be nicer still if we didn't *need* to care, if the world didn't require our care. But since it does need our care, one must just do the best one can.

Of course both Confucius and Bill Bailey inhabited lives radically harder than my own. This is, in no small part, why I appeal to them as I consider what can carry me through as I struggle to be well-mannered. I am set into a world in which prizing my sociality and humanity are rendered more challenging by the division, strife, and contention that characterize our present civic and political life. I struggle to maintain the "faith" and preserve longings for a world less beset by the nickel-and-diming cruelties that can leave me, and many, misanthropic and ready to give up on shared civic life. Unlike Confucius and Bailey, the warlords and combat I encounter are figurative. Appealing to their fragile hopes, developed in conditions far worse than mine, thus has the effect of usefully shaming me in my own inconstancies. After all, to enact my own longings I just have to *talk*, to engage optimistically and generously with those who share the world I inhabit. Under the power of Confucius's and Bailey's examples, there is something shamefully un-grown-up in deciding to do otherwise. But apart from enjoining me to greater maturity about the challenges I face, Confucius and Bailey evince an attitude I can seek to cultivate in my own disappointments.

In Confucius and Bailey, I find consolation for the more modest disappointments of seeking sociality through the hopeful optimism good manners recommend. I inhabit a world riven with petty unkindnesses, small symbolic injustices, and myriad affronting trifles. I wish it weren't so, yet cannot, under my own powers, make it decisively otherwise. I can, to be sure, react to it with my own small generosities, justices, and kinder trifles, and these *will* matter to some who receive them. When they do not more widely matter, when the larger world persists as it is in spite of my effort, I can nonetheless abide in the comfort of the longing itself. That is, sometimes wanting what you cannot have yet wanting it anyway is part of feeling its value, part of being enlivened and sustained by it. Indeed, where our sociality is concerned, this form of longing seems especially significant and important. For, as Bailey attests, not liking the world you inhabit and seeking to alter it in whatever modest ways one can reaches for a different future for others, "call it the history of the human race, if you want to."

If there is even a small chance that my persisting in a hopeful life that entails some disappointment will make such disappointments fewer for others later, that is an outcome I can indeed prize. In this regard, disappointments can even work as a kind of motivational power. For my *not* liking the frustration of hope can spur me to reach for that future that Bailey does, imagining a world sometime hence when someone will have it *better*. Being bound to humanity as it presently is, staying in the struggle, can for me at least find consolation in a future humanity to which I am also bound, a future humanity I want to have it better than we do. This is no grand promise of great reward for me or how my own life will go. Yet it does just enough, consoles just enough, to help me persist. In the shadow of figures like Confucius and Bill Bailey, I can continue to extend the vulnerable hand of sociality, take whatever "beatings" that entails, yet still imagine that later day with a quiet, consoling, "Glory to me, or somethin' like that."

NOTES

Chapter 1

1. Michael Curtin, "A Question of Manners: Status and Gender in Etiquette and Courtesy," *Journal of Modern History* 57.3 (1985): 395–423.
2. Curtin, "A Question of Manners," 418.
3. Cheshire Calhoun, "The Virtue of Civility," *Philosophy and Public Affairs* 29 (2000): 259.

Chapter 2

1. A flurry of memes arose after Richard Spencer, an alt-right leader, was filmed as he was punched during protests upon the inauguration of Donald Trump in January 2016. Multiple celebratory memes appeared, featuring footage of the punch set to music, and several (implicitly or explicitly) justified "punching a Nazi." For a news account of the event and the memes it generated, see Liam Stack, "Attack on Alt-Right Leader Has Internet Asking: Is It O.K. to Punch a Nazi?," *New York Times*, January 21, 2016, online edition: https://www.nytimes.com/2017/01/21/us/politics/richard-spencer-punched-attack.html?_r=0. Accessed September 19, 2018.
2. Calhoun, "The Virtue of Civility," 252.

Chapter 3

1. Edward Slingerland, *Trying Not to Try: The Art and Science of Spontaneity* (New York: Crown Publishers, 2014), 64.

2. Judith Martin, *Miss Manners Rescues Civilization, from Sexual Harassment, Frivolous Lawsuits, Dissing, and Other Lapses in Civility* (New York: Crown Publishers, 1996), 3.

3. Plato, *The Apology*, in John M. Cooper, ed., *Plato: Complete Works* (Indianapolis: Hackett, 1997), 17a–18a.

4. Jean-Jacques Rousseau, "Discourse on the Sciences and the Arts," in John T. Scott, ed. and trans., *The Major Political Writings of Jean-Jacques Rousseau* (Chicago: University of Chicago Press, 2012), 13.

5. Rousseau, "Discourse," 13.

6. Qtd. in James Boswell, *Life of Johnson* (Oxford: Oxford University Press, 1953), 188.

7. Philip Dormer Stanhope Chesterfield, *Lord Chesterfield's Letters*, David Robert, ed. (New York: Oxford University Press, 1992), 72.

8. Chesterfield, *Lord Chesterfield's Letters*, 70 (emphasis in original).

9. Martin, *Miss Manners Rescues Civilization*, 5.

10. For the curious reader, Martin replied to this query by noting that we need not all have the same pleasures in life and that so long as we take care to seek them in appropriate contexts, there shouldn't be a problem: "The prospects of riding in the back of a pickup truck with six cans of beer sloshing around in her stomach and no underwear is not, as you have astutely guessed, her idea of a rollicking good time. But she has no objection to it being yours" (Martin, *Miss Manners Rescues Civilization*, 5).

11. Joel Kupperman, *Classic Asian Philosophy* (New York: Oxford University Press, 2007), 119.

12. Kupperman, *Classic Asian Philosophy*, 122.

Chapter 4

1. Philippa Foot, "Morality as a System of Hypothetical Imperatives," *Philosophical Review* 81.3 (1972): 314.

2. Qtd. in Calhoun, "The Virtue of Civility," 256.

3. Sarah Buss, "Appearing Respectful: The Moral Significance of Manners," *Ethics* 109.4 (1999): 802.

4. Xunzi, *The Complete Text*, trans. Eric Hutton (Princeton: Princeton University Press, 2014), 217. Hereafter cited as "Hutton."

5. "Area Baby Doesn't Have Any Friends," *The Onion* 41–46 (November 16, 2005). Available at http://www.theonion.com/content/node/42599 Accessed February 26, 2018.

6. *Analects* 1.1. All citations to the *Analects* are from Robert Eno, trans., *The Analects of Confucius*, 2015, published as open access online at http://www.indiana.edu/~p374/Analects_of_Confucius_(Eno-2015).pdf. Accessed May 1, 2018. For ease of reference, citations are given in the customary format,

listing chapter and passage number. Where I have modified Eno's translations, I include this in the relevant notes.

7. *Analects* 4.21.

8. *Analects* 16.5.

9. *Analects* 9.12.

10. Mark Edward Lewis, *Sanctioned Violence in Early China* (Albany: State University of New York Press, 1989), 36.

11. Roger T. Ames, trans., *Sunzi: The Art of Warfare* (New York: Ballantine Books, 1993), 32–34.

12. *Analects* 15.2.

13. *Shiji* 87, in Sima Qian, *Records of the Grand Historian: Qin Dynasty*, trans. Burton Watson (New York: Columbia University Press, 1993), 206.

14. Hutton, 267.

15. Hutton, 268.

16. Hutton, 267.

17. Hutton, 268–269.

18. Xunzi uses this term throughout chapter 23 in characterizing the amendment of our bad natures.

19. Hutton, 225.

20. Hutton, 268.

21. Multiple news articles following the election cited the various ways in which populations in the United States divide along multiple vectors, including political views, race, and income. For one discussion of these demographic "bubbles," see Derek Thompson, "Everybody's in a Bubble and That's a Problem," *The Atlantic*, January 25, 2017. Available at https://www.theatlantic.com/business/archive/2017/01/america-bubbles/514385/. Accessed February 13, 2018.

Chapter 5

1. *Analects* 2.4; translation modified.

2. *Analects* 12.1; translation modified.

3. David Wong, "Cultivating the Self in Concert with Others," in Amy Olberding, ed., *Dao Companion to the Analects* (New York: Springer Press, 2014), 183.

4. *Analects* 4.17.

5. *Analects* 4.3.

6. *Analects* 14.29.

7. Sam Gosling, *Snoop: What Your Stuff Says about You* (New York: Basic Books, 2008).

8. For discussion of the role and accuracy of stereotypes, see Gosling, *Snoop*, chapter 7. Part of Gosling's project concerns sussing out just which of the stereotypes we employ in reading stuff have higher accuracy—that is, which

associations between stuff and people remark empirically measurable traits about populations. While some of our stereotypes do appear to have greater accuracy, I don't focus on this element of his work here for two reasons: (1) I am concerned with how we read individuals, and the group trends remarked by Gosling are less useful on this score, and (2) as Gosling notes, the stereotypes with higher accuracy are not predictable in ways we would expect, nor does confidence about stereotyping judgment track its accuracy.

9. Gosling, *Snoop*, 164.

10. Martin, *Miss Manners Rescues Civilization*, 51.

11. Jennifer Van Evra, "Sarah Silverman's Response to a Twitter Troll Is a Master Class in Compassion," *q*, the blog of CBC/Radio Canada, January 3, 2018. Available at http://www.cbc.ca/radio/q/blog/sarah-silverman-s-response-to-a-twitter-troll-is-a-master-class-in-compassion-1.4471337. Accessed January 21, 2018.

12. *Analects* 12.19.

13. *Analects* 2.1.

14. *Analects* 4.25.

15. *Analects* 9.14.

16. Hutton, 2–3.

17. Hutton, 276.

18. Hutton, 19.

19. Elaine Hatfield, John T. Cacioppo, and Richard L. Rapson, *Emotional Contagion* (New York: Cambridge University Press, 1994), 5.

20. Hatfield, Cacioppo, and Rapson, *Emotional Contagion*, 5.

21. William James, "The Will to Believe," in James, *Essays in Pragmatism* (New York: Hafner, 1969), 104.

22. James, "The Will to Believe," 104.

Chapter 6

1. George Washington, *Rules of Civility and Decent Behavior* (New York: MJF Books, 2007).

2. Martin, *Miss Manners Rescues Civilization*, 30.

3. Hutton, 204.

4. Chenyang Li, "*Li* as Cultural Grammar: The Relation between *Li* and *Ren* in the *Analects*," *Philosophy East and West* 57.3 (2007): 311–329.

5. Robert Eno, *The Confucian Creation of Heaven* (Albany: State University of New York Press, 1990), 31. Eno here uses "ritual" to translate *li*, but I have here substituted "etiquette."

6. Herbert Fingarette, *Confucius: The Secular as Sacred* (New York: Waveland Press, 1998), 9.

7. Kelly M. Epley, "Care Ethics and Confucianism: Caring through *Li*," *Hypatia* 30.4 (2015): 891.

8. Hutton, 10.

9. Hutton, 2.

10. Hutton, 232.

11. Slingerland, *Trying Not to Try*, 28–32.

12. Slingerland, *Trying Not to Try*, 32.

13. Slingerland, *Trying Not to Try*, 67.

14. Tonya Jacobi and Dylan Schweers, "Legal Scholarship Highlight: Justice, Interrupted—Gender, Ideology and Seniority at the Supreme Court," *Scotusblog*. Available at http://www.scotusblog.com/2017/04/legal-scholarship-highlight-justice-interrupted-gender-ideology-seniority-supreme-court/. Accessed April 29, 2017.

15. Richard Duffy, introduction to Emily Post, *Etiquette: In Society, in Business, in Politics, and at Home* (New York: Funk and Wagnalls Company, 1923), x.

Chapter 7

1. Hutton, 10.

2. Remarks about Confucius's bodily habits are sprinkled throughout the *Analects*, but are most concentrated in Book 10.

3. I am indebted to my teacher Roger Ames for, years ago, suggesting this interpretation of the *Analects*, an interpretation I only fully appreciated once I had my own teenager.

4. I borrow and adapt this example from Karen Stohr, who uses it to illuminate a Kantian version of manners and the problem of line-breaking. See Stohr, *On Manners* (New York: Routledge, 2012), 12–13.

5. Xunzi emphasizes the power of manners to truncate some dispositions while expanding others, and being well-mannered is often a matter of reducing the more raw and base dispositions while extending the more noble and humane ones. See, e.g., Hutton, 210.

6. Sigal G. Barsade, "The Ripple Effect: Emotional Contagion and Its Influence on Group Behavior," *Administrative Science Quarterly* 47.4 (2002): 667.

7. Barsade, "The Ripple Effect," 656.

8. George Yancy, *Black Bodies, White Gazes: The Continuing Significance of Race* (New York: Rowman and Littlefield, 2008), 2.

9. Yancy, *Black Bodies, White Gazes*, 4.

10. Brent Staples, qtd. in Claude Steele, *Whistling Vivaldi: How Stereotypes Affect Us and What We Can Do* (New York: Norton, 2011), 6.

11. Hutton, 5.

NOTES

12. Images from the series and Morris-Cafiero's description of their origins may be found at her personal website: http://www.haleymorriscafiero.com. Accessed March 15, 2018.

13. David Rosenberg, "She Tried to Create a Dialogue about Fat-Shaming and Got Fat-Shamed. That Gave Her a Great New Idea," *Slate*, March 3, 2016. Available at http://www.slate.com/blogs/behold/2016/03/03/haley_morris_cafiero_s_wait_watchers_photos_examine_of_how_we_perceive_body.html. Accessed February 19, 2018.

Chapter 8

1. *Analects* 17.20.
2. Bryan Van Norden, trans., *Mengzi* (Indianapolis: Hackett, 2008), 1A17.
3. Karen Stohr offers a helpful analysis of what expert judgment includes in Stohr, *On Manners*, chapter 3.
4. The trouble with following the role model offered by the sages among us is too complex to treat in detail here. However, a quick way to illuminate the basic trouble is but to recognize that in many circumstances that might prompt me to ask, "What would Confucius do?" the most *accurate* answer would be, "Well, Confucius would never have gotten himself into such a stupid spot."
5. Hutton, 138.
6. *Analects* 12.18.
7. *Analects* 12.19.
8. The full transcript of Michelle Obama's speech may be found at the *Washington Post* website: https://www.washingtonpost.com/news/post-politics/wp/2016/07/26/transcript-read-michelle-obamas-full-speech-from-the-2016-dnc/?utm_term=.03226ffe83d7. Posted July 26, 2016. Accessed March 3, 2018.
9. For the curious: My student did not walk out of church in protest, but stayed in his seat and later discussed the sermon with his grandparents.
10. Calhoun, "The Virtue of Civility," 275.

Chapter 9

1. Linda Zagzebski offers a distinction that is implicit in my discussion, that between a life we find desirable and a life we find admirable. As she notes, our use of "good life" often combines these in uneven and unclear ways. Much of what I describe here can be cast as the ways an admirable life can end up sacrificing just the sorts of comfort and contentment that accompany a desirable life. See Linda Trinkaus Zagzebski, "The Admirable Life and the Desirable

Life," in Timothy Chappell, ed., *Values and Virtues* (Oxford: Oxford University Press, 2006).

2. *Analects* 11.26.

3. Of the early Chinese philosophers recommending this, the Yangists are the most direct, though we know of their claims only indirectly, through references to them in other texts. Strains of this view appear in *Zhuangzi*, traditionally considered a Daoist text, and the philosopher Zhuangzi, for example, claims that it would be better to be a tortoise "dragging its tail in the mud" than get involved in politics. A. C. Graham, trans. *Chuang-tzu: The Inner Chapters* (Indianapolis: Hackett, 1981), 122.

4. Studs Terkel, *The Good War: An Oral History of World War II* (New York: MJF Books, 1984), 98.

5. Terkel, *The Good War*, 102–103.

WORKS CITED

Ames, Roger T., trans. *Sunzi: The Art of Warfare*. New York: Ballantine Books, 1993.

"Area Baby Doesn't Have Any Friends." *The Onion* 41–46 (November 16, 2005). Available at http://www.theonion.com/content/node/42599. Accessed February 26, 2018.

Barsade, Sigal G. "The Ripple Effect: Emotional Contagion and Its Influence on Group Behavior." *Administrative Science Quarterly* 47.4 (2002): 644–675.

Boswell, James. *Life of Johnson*. Oxford: Oxford University Press, 1953.

Buss, Sarah. "Appearing Respectful: The Moral Significance of Manners." *Ethics* 109.4 (1999): 795–826.

Calhoun, Cheshire. "The Virtue of Civility." *Philosophy and Public Affairs* 29 (2000): 251–275.

Curtin, Michael. "A Question of Manners: Status and Gender in Etiquette and Courtesy." *Journal of Modern History* 57.3 (1985): 395–423.

Chesterfield, Philip Dormer Stanhope. *Lord Chesterfield's Letters*. David Robert, ed. New York: Oxford University Press, 1992.

Duffy, Richard. Introduction to Emily Post, *Etiquette: In Society, in Business, in Politics, and at Home*. New York: Funk and Wagnalls Company, 1923.

Eno, Robert. *The Confucian Creation of Heaven*. Albany: State University of New York Press, 1990.

Epley, Kelly M. "Care Ethics and Confucianism: Caring through *Li*." *Hypatia* 30.4 (2015): 881–896.

Fingarette, Herbert. *Confucius: The Secular as Sacred*. New York: Waveland Press, 1998.

Foot, Philippa. "Morality as a System of Hypothetical Imperatives." *Philosophical Review* 81.3 (1972): 305–316.

Gosling, Sam. *Snoop: What Your Stuff Says about You.* New York: Basic Books, 2008.

Graham, A. C., trans. *Chuang-tzu: The Inner Chapters.* Indianapolis: Hackett, 1981.

Hatfield, Elaine, John T. Cacioppo, and Richard L. Rapson. *Emotional Contagion.* New York: Cambridge University Press, 1994.

Jacobi, Tonya and Dylan Schweers. "Legal Scholarship Highlight: Justice, Interrupted—Gender, Ideology and Seniority at the Supreme Court." *Scotusblog,* April 5, 2017. Available at http://www.scotusblog.com/2017/04/legal-scholarship-highlight-justice-interrupted-gender-ideology-seniority-supreme-court/. Accessed April 29, 2017.

James, William. *The Will to Believe.* In James, *Essays in Pragmatism.* New York: Hafner, 1969.

Kupperman, Joel. *Classic Asian Philosophy.* New York: Oxford University Press, 2007.

Lewis, Mark Edward. *Sanctioned Violence in Early China.* Albany: State University of New York Press, 1989.

Li, Chenyang. "*Li* as Cultural Grammar: The Relation between *Li* and *Ren* in the *Analects.*" *Philosophy East and West* 57.3 (2007): 311–329.

Martin, Judith. *Miss Manners Rescues Civilization, from Sexual Harassment, Frivolous Lawsuits, Dissing, and Other Lapses in Civility.* New York: Crown Publishers, 1996.

Plato. *The Apology.* In John M. Cooper, ed., *Plato: Complete Works.* Indianapolis: Hackett, 1997.

Rosenberg, David. "She Tried to Create a Dialogue about Fat-Shaming and Got Fat-Shamed. That Gave Her a Great New Idea." *Slate,* March 3, 2016. Available at http://www.slate.com/blogs/behold/2016/03/03/haley_morris_cafiero_s_wait_watchers_photos_examine_of_how_we_perceive_body.html.

Rousseau, Jean-Jacques. "Discourse on the Sciences and the Arts." In John T. Scott, ed., *The Major Political Writings of Jean-Jacques Rousseau.* Chicago: University of Chicago Press, 2012.

Sima Qian. *Records of the Grand Historian: Qin Dynasty.* Trans. Burton Watson. New York: Columbia University Press, 1993.

Slingerland, Edward. *Trying Not to Try: The Art and Science of Spontaneity.* New York: Crown Publishers, 2014.

Steele, Claude. *Whistling Vivaldi: How Stereotypes Affect Us and What We Can Do.* New York: Norton, 2011.

Stewart, B. D. and B. K. Payne. "Bringing Automatic Stereotyping under Control: Implementation Intentions as Efficient Means of Thought Control." *Personality and Social Psychology Bulletin* 34 (2008): 1332–1345.

Stohr, Karen. *On Manners.* New York: Routledge, 2012.

Terkel, Studs. *The Good War: An Oral History of World War II.* New York: MJF Books, 1984.

Thompson, Derek. "Everybody's in a Bubble and That's a Problem." *The Atlantic*, January 25, 2017. Available at https://www.theatlantic.com/business/archive/2017/01/america-bubbles/514385/ Accessed March 4, 2018.

Van Evra, Jennifer. "Sarah Silverman's Response to a Twitter Troll Is a Master Class in Compassion." *q*, the blog of CBC/Radio Canada, January 3, 2018. Available at http://www.cbc.ca/radio/q/blog/sarah-silverman-s-response-to-a-twitter-troll-is-a-master-class-in-compassion-1.4471337. Accessed January 21, 2018.

Van Norden, Bryan, trans. *Mengzi*. Indianapolis: Hackett, 2008.

Washington, George. *Rules of Civility and Decent Behavior*. New York: MJF Books, 2007.

Wong, David. "Cultivating the Self in Concert with Others." In Amy Olberding, ed., *Dao Companion to the Analects*. New York: Springer Press, 2014.

Xunzi. *The Complete Text*. Trans. Eric Hutton. Princeton: Princeton University Press, 2014.

Yancy, George. *Black Bodies, White Gazes: The Continuing Significance of Race*. New York: Rowman and Littlefield, 2008.

Zagzebski, Linda Trinkaus. "The Admirable Life and the Desirable Life." In Timothy Chappell, ed., *Values and Virtues*. Oxford: Oxford University Press, 2006.

INDEX